THE NEVILLE SITE

8,000 YEARS AT AMOSKEAG

Peabody Museum Monographs
Harvard University • Cambridge, Massachusetts
Number 4

THE NEVILLE SITE
8,000 Years at Amoskeag
MANCHESTER, NEW HAMPSHIRE

DENA FERRAN DINCAUZE

Published with the Assistance of the
New Hampshire Archeological Society

Peabody Museum of Archaeology and Ethnology
Harvard University • Cambridge, Massachusetts
1976

This book is a facsimile edition authorized by the
Peabody Museum Press of Harvard University.
It is produced on acid-free archival paper,
which meets the requirements of ANSI/NISO Z39.48-1992.

Facsimile created by Acme Bookbinding,
Charlestown, Massachusetts.

Facsimile printing 2005

Second facsimile printing 2008

Preface

The excavation of the Neville site in 1968 was a major event in the archaeological history of New England. At one stroke the known duration of continuous occupation in the region was extended by three thousand years, and very close, early connections with the Southeast were demonstrated. Perspectives into the past were thus significantly deepened and widened, and through them New England's prehistoric relationships with the rest of the East could be better understood.

None of this would have occurred without the faith, dedication, and labor of Peter McLane and his co-workers, Kenneth Rhodes and Emmanuel Valavane. They worked carefully and diligently through the spring and summer of 1968, under pressure of the approach of bridge construction crews. They persevered in the face of initial skepticism about the significance of their discoveries, skepticism which derived its strength from paradigms severely challenged by the artifacts stratified below the familiar Late Archaic assemblages. Finally, their generous gift to the Peabody Museum at Harvard University of the entire collection and records made possible the study reported here.

The significance of the site to the cultural heritage of New Hampshire was recognized by the trustees of the Norwin S. and Elizabeth N. Bean Foundation of the New Hampshire Charitable Fund in Concord, who awarded Peter McLane a grant in support of radiocarbon dating. A second grant, to the Peabody Museum, supported the initial processing and the greater part of the analytical work on the collection. The preparation of this report, including the artifact analysis, was supported by the National Science Foundation.

The administration of these several grants involved a number of individuals and the facilities of several institutions whose aid was indispensable. I am grateful for the support and encouragement provided by Professor Stephen Williams, Director of the Peabody Museum at Harvard, Professor June Collins of the Anthropology Department of SUNY College at Buffalo, Professor Elmer Harp of the Anthropology Department of Dartmouth College, Virginia Plisko of the Manchester Historic

Association, and the Research Foundation of the State University of New York.

I accept full responsibility for the interpretations and conclusions presented in this report. In doing so, I acknowledge gratefully the major contributions made to the work by others. The labor of the excavators was the beginning of a task which involved the time and effort of many people, who gave freely of their skills and knowledge simply because, as Albert Spaulding remarked in a similar context, they "enjoy comprehending."

During and after the fieldwork, the excavators were aided by Eugene Winter and Polly McLane, who have since supplied additional background information for various aspects of the research. Students and colleagues at Harvard University, SUNY College at Buffalo, and the University of Massachusetts have enriched the study and lightened the burden of the work by their efforts, skills, and insights. While not all can be thanked individually, special recognition is due to R. Michael Gramly, Peter Thomas, and Ned Librock, whose contributions were outstanding. My understanding of the Pleistocene geology of the Amoskeag locale owes much to conversations with Carl Koteff of the U.S. Geological Survey; the interpretations presented here are mostly my own, and he is absolved from any responsibility for them.

All of the illustrations except figure 1 were prepared by James Kasprzyk of Cheektowaga, New York. The locational map was drawn by Symme Burstein at the Peabody Museum. The plates were photographed by E. James Schifferli of Cheektowaga, New York, except for plates 1 and 2, which are derived from photographs taken by the excavators.

And finally, for emphasis, I wish to thank the John Neville family, who gave consent for the digging that started it all.

D.F.D.
Amherst, Massachusetts
July 1974

Contents

Figures

Plates

Tables

Introduction

HISTORY AND LOCATION OF THE SITE

The Merrimack River is formed in east-central New Hampshire by the junction of the Pemigwasset and Winnipesaukee rivers. The postglacial Merrimack River has not regained its ancient bedrock valley; it flows through old proglacial lake beds and other glacial deposits, occasionally cutting down to bedrock sills. A series of falls and rapids has therefore developed along its course. The largest of these, the Amoskeag Falls, is a series of chutes and rapids, bordered by steep bluffs, in the northern part of Manchester, New Hampshire.

The Amoskeag area was a famous spring fishery before power dams blocked the stream in the middle of the nineteenth century. The name is derived from the Indian word for "fishing place," a name the English colonists never improved upon. Shad, salmon, alewives, and lampreys ran the falls during the spring spawning season in overwhelming numbers. In the seventeenth century, Amoskeag was the site for general convocations of Indians who gathered to fish, feast, and celebrate for the duration of the runs. The importance of the area prehistorically has been demonstrated by the large collections of artifacts gathered there during the last two hundred years, although none has been published in any useful detail and most have been lost or dispersed without record (Willoughby 1935, figures 37h, 50j, 130; Potter 1856, pp. 29-30; Moorehead 1931, pp. 59-66, 69, 70; Marshall 1942). The Manchester Historical Association maintains some important collections from the area.

The Neville site lay on the east (left) bank of the Merrimack, immediately north of the lip of Amoskeag Falls (fig. 1). It was located at the northern end of a postglacial river terrace which provided living space below the bluff top and well above normal flood levels. It was near the northern extremity of the Indian occupation area of the eastern bank, so far as that is known. Immediately east and about forty feet higher stood the Governor Smyth estate, long famous for the abundance of its prehistoric relics (Moorehead 1931, pp. 62, 71).

The Neville site entered history as part of the farm of Archibald Stark, one of the original "Scotch-Irish" settlers of modern Manchester.

1

Stark built a house near Amoskeag in 1736, which passed after 1758 to his son John. John Stark earned fame for his victorious command of New Hampshire troops at the Battle of Bennington, Vermont, in 1777. He returned to the farm after service, and eventually sold it in 1801. The Stark house stood in its original location until 1968, when it was moved to avoid demolition.

In 1967, the Neville property on which the excavation took place was bounded on the east by River Street, on the south by West Salmon Street, and on the west by a railroad embankment (fig. 1). River Street follows the route of a major north-south road which passed just east of the Stark house from before 1754, when it was formally recorded (Potter 1856, p. 692). West Salmon Street, which separated the archaeological site from the Stark homestead, was built in connection with the Amoskeag Falls Bridge between 1839 and 1842. The Neville house was erected as a tollhouse for the bridge in 1842 and was so used until the bridge became a public way in 1853 (ibid., p. 712). Subsequently, the house was rented until purchased in 1925 by John Neville, who lived there until the land was taken in 1967 for the new bridge (Manchester Historic Association archives). The Concord Railroad line on the western edge of the archaeological site was constructed on the modern floodplain below the site between 1835 and 1842, when it was opened for travel. Thus, the bounds of the site as they existed in 1967 had been established in 1842 and, except for limited road and bridge improvements since then, had remained essentially unchanged.

This is the more remarkable in that the great industrial development of Manchester took place immediately south of the Stark homestead. John Stark had built the first water mill at Amoskeag around 1760, to saw lumber. A barge canal and other mills were later constructed downstream on the eastern shore. There, in midnineteenth century, the Amoskeag millyard was built as an exemplar of the technical and social achievements of the Industrial Revolution (ibid., pp. 560-562). In the process, it destroyed an extensive record of the technical and social achievements of another people and other times. However, north of West Salmon Street a little piece of land was buried under cinders, construction debris, and dirt excavated from the tollhouse cellar hole.

HISTORY OF THE INVESTIGATION

In 1967, the New Hampshire Department of Public Works and Highways announced plans to rebuild the Amoskeag bridge. The new span would be both wider and higher than the old and would reach the eastern shore a short distance north of the old bridgehead. Relocation of West Salmon Street would destroy part of the Governor Smyth garden grounds, and the bridgehead would engulf the Neville and Stark properties on the terrace below.

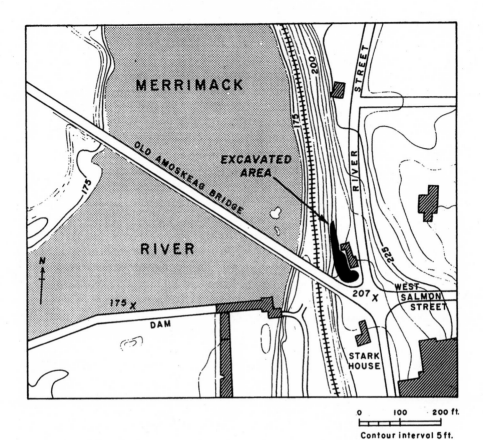

Contour interval 5 ft.

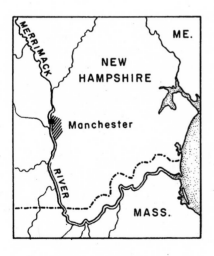

FIGURE 1

LOCATION OF

THE NEVILLE SITE

MANCHESTER,

NEW HAMPSHIRE, 1968

The New Hampshire Archeological Society mobilized for salvage excavation at the Smyth site, which was also threatened by the expansion of parking facilities for business use. Officers of the Society directed a crew of volunteers who excavated through the summers of 1967 and 1968. Their discoveries in 1967 established the importance of the Smyth site and attracted considerable public support and attention. Among the volunteers recruited at the site was Peter McLane, who lived nearby. Pete was among the small number of regular volunteers who showed up consistently for work during long summer evenings and weekends. His growing enthusiasm for the job, and the closeness of his residence, made him impatient with the limited hours during which supervised volunteer excavation could be conducted. In addition, he was concerned that the Society was testing such a limited part of the area that would be destroyed by the bridge.

Spurred by his conviction that the Amoskeag locale held unique potential for revealing New Hampshire prehistory, he decided to work on his own in an additional area. Toward the end of the 1967 excavation season, he obtained permission to test on the lower terrace, in the Neville family's yard, where he excavated two test pits. The depth of the deposits and the space available there encouraged him to plan a major excavation in 1968.

Initially, Pete dug alone or with the help of three sons. Eventually, he was joined by Ken Rhodes and Emmanuel Valavane, who worked under his direction, with comparable dedication. Working weekends, evenings, and holidays through the spring and summer, the three men excavated thirty-four pits, each five feet square and six feet deep (fig. 2). By the completion of the first five squares it was obvious that something remarkable was being revealed. The upper three feet contained an assortment of typical southern New England artifacts, a confusing jumble of projectile points and potsherds. The lowest three feet, however, contained a more limited range of artifacts, most of unfamiliar styles.

Curious about the strange lower levels, Pete turned to radiocarbon analysis. He chose a small sample which came from the base of the deposits in association with a stemmed projectile point. The age, 5,385 ±380 years, was one of the oldest then reported for New England Archaic materials. There ensued a series of consultations with northeastern archaeologists, amateur and professional. The consultations were conducted at pitside and over Pete's dining table, where artifacts were laid out by square and level. The discussions confirmed the excavators' convictions that their material was of unusual significance.

Excavations ended in September, 1968, as mechanized earth-moving for the bridge began. The digging over, a second charcoal sample was tested in response to the suggestion that the first sample probably minimized the true age of the cultural material at the base of the sequence.

The second sample was 7,015±160 years old, implying a major extension of New England's cultural chronology.

His faith thus dramatically vindicated, Pete accepted prime responsibility for preparing the report. He was awarded a grant, for additional radiocarbon analyses, which was administered through Dartmouth College of which he was an alumnus. Through the interest of Professor Elmer Harp of the Anthropology Department, it was arranged to have students make a preliminary analysis of the artifacts. Their brief study was inconclusive. Pete's report was barely past the initial outline stage when he was stricken with terminal illness. Aware that he would not complete the study, he and his associates offered the collection and records to Harvard University, requesting the present author to analyze and report the data.

STUDY METHODS

At the time when I assumed responsibility for the Neville project, the site itself had been destroyed. Excavation for the bridge footings lowered the surface of the site several feet, obliterating remnant cultural deposits there. The records and materials collected in 1968 comprise all that we will ever have from the site, and they are the basis for the report which follows.

I accepted the responsibility for analysis and reporting because of the unique structure and significance of the site. It remains to this date the thickest series of archaeological deposits known in New England, where most sites are shallower than the plow zones which effaced them. The clarity of the cultural stratigraphy is also unequaled in the region, convincingly demonstrating the relative positions of at least six distinct Archaic complexes. The lower levels of the site enclosed an exceptionally rich and detailed record of Middle Archaic cultures, whose very existence was contested before the excavation of this site.

The study was undertaken to achieve three specific goals; no exhaustive consideration of the data has been attempted. The goals were: (1) to demonstrate the validity of the stratigraphic sequence, (2) to describe and date the cultural sequence at the site, and (3) to define the patterns of the site utilization through time.

Procedures

The collection was received at the Peabody Museum, Harvard University, early in 1970 (accession 970-12). Most of the artifacts had been separated by the excavators from the debitage and rough stone tools and were labeled with square and level designations. The bulk of the materials arrived in level bags, uncatalogued. As a result, a detailed accessions catalogue was compiled at the Museum, which could also serve as a field catalogue.

The natural stratigraphy of the site is described and documented in chapter 1. The records available for the stratigraphic study are detailed there, as are the methods by which the records were compiled and interpreted.

The artifact attribute analysis and the classification reported in chapter 2 were the primary methods chosen for achieving the second and third goals, those of culture sequence and site utilization. The artifact studies were completed during the summer of 1973, in the Anthropology Laboratory at State University College in Buffalo, New York. Artifacts of the early historical period, from Stratum 2, were accidentally excluded from the materials shipped to Buffalo, so that they were not available for detailed analysis. Anglo-American cultural remains at the site are therefore summarized only superficially in this report.

1
Natural History

GEOLOGY AND ENVIRONMENT

Topography and Structure

Manchester lies within the New England physiographic province of Fenneman, on the boundary between the Seaboard Lowland and the New England Upland sections (Fenneman 1938, pl. I). Elevations near Manchester are below 600 feet, and below 350 feet within a mile of Amoskeag Falls. The Falls themselves mark the northern limit of the Merrimack lowland, a wedge-shaped area widening to the south, which is below 200 feet. The Merrimack lowland is the only area in New Hampshire outside of the narrow coastal lowland which is so close to sea level (Billings 1956, pp. 1-4).

The bedrock under Manchester is part of the Hillsboro plutonic series of Middle Paleozoic age. In the Amoskeag area, bedrock outcrops only where it has been exposed by the river at the falls; elsewhere, it is deeply buried by glacial and glaciolacustrine deposits of Pleistocene age.

Pleistocene sediments filled the preglacial Merrimack valley to depths of 100 feet in some places (Goldthwait et al. 1951, p. 22). During the retreat of the Wisconsin ice sheet, one or more glacial lakes formed in the valley between the ice front on the north and temporary dams of glacial debris downsteam. When the lake drained, water flowing south over the lake bottom beds revived the Merrimack River which, remaining within its old valley, cut a new channel into the unconsolidated Pleistocene sediments. Amoskeag Falls is only one of many falls and rapids formed since then as the downcutting river exposed bedrock sills at many places along its course.

Modern Climate and Soils

Manchester is 35 miles inland from the Atlantic Ocean, but its climate is affected very little by marine influences. It has the warm summers and cold winters of continental climates, with the intensification of seasonal extremes which is typical of valley climates. Winter temperatures average

7

a few degrees Fahrenheit below freezing; summer temperatures average around 70°F. Short term variations of temperature as great as 30 degrees in twenty-four hours are not unusual (Simmons et al. 1953, p.6). The frost-free season extends from mid-May to late September, with the normal six months' growing season beginning a month earlier and lasting a month later. Precipitation shows no marked seasonality, although there is a relatively dry season in late summer, and periods of prolonged wetness tend to occur near the equinoxes.

Soils in the Manchester area are mainly of the Brown Podzolic group, with some localized Podzols. Brown Podzolic soils develop on well-drained soils under mixed forest cover.

Recent Vegetation

Southeastern New Hampshire is within the zone of Transitional forest — mixed hardwood and conifer associations which occupy a broad belt between the southern deciduous forest and the coniferous boreal forest of higher latitudes. In the Manchester area, the native forest of the seventeenth and eighteenth centuries consisted of northern hardwoods and was broken by almost pure stands of white pine on the driest sandy soils. Northern red oak, yellow birch, American beech, and sugar maple were among the most important hardwoods (Simmons et al. 1953, p. 103). The Manchester historian, Potter, confirms this association with some differences for Amoskeag, recording that "The north part of the city was originally covered with a heavy growth of oak, maple, ash and white pine, while the banks of the rivers . . . were covered by a heavy growth of yellow and white pine" (Potter 1856, p. 634).

Recent Wild Fauna

The fauna of the Manchester area was dominated by the Virginia deer, which thrived in the forest edge communities of the river valleys and pond margins. Moose and black bear were the other large animals. Mountain lion, wildcat, lynx, wolf, fisher, beaver, and otter were listed by Potter in 1856 as current or former residents of Manchester. Potter spared his reader a longer enumeration by concluding evasively that "other animals of common and less notoriety, were formerly often found within our city limits" (ibid., p. 635). The now extinct heath hen was prominent among game birds. Quail and partridge were also mentioned. The fishery at Amoskeag, however, was the greatest protein resource of the area. In May and June, especially, anadromous fish ran up the falls in overwhelming numbers. Shad were most numerous, Atlantic salmon, the largest and most succulent, and alewives, important for their numbers but probably the least sought by man. In addition, lampreys were present in significant quantities (Bailey 1938, pp. 155, 162, 164; Potter 1856, p. 636). There are historical records of large sturgeon caught at the falls (Bailey 1938, p. 162). So rich was the fishing at Amoskeag in the early eighteenth century that the proprietorship of the area was bitterly contested for many years, with the Massachusetts Bay Colony prominent among the claimants (Potter 1856, pp. 640-641).

Distant Resources

In addition to the local advantages, prehistoric residents of Amoskeag were able to draw on the resources of several other habitats because of their strategic location on the Merrimack, which made travel relatively easy to the north and south. Upstream where the Merrimack is formed from the junction of two rivers, the tributary valleys provided access to the White Mountains via the Pemigwasset River and to Lake Winnipesaukee via the river of the same name. North and southeast of Lake Winnipesaukee are the Ossipee and Copple Crown mountains, where volcanic rocks with good flaking qualities can be obtained. Near the mouth of the Merrimack, about 65 miles downstream, were rich estuarine and coastal habitats and more outcrops of useful fine-grained volcanic rocks.

Structure and Depositional History of the Neville Terrace

The glacial lake at Manchester, which left bedded deposits up to 260 feet in elevation, was drained around 13,000 years ago (C. Koteff, personal communication). The revived Merrimack River began to cut its channel into the soft sediments, swinging laterally in the course of the downcutting. Terraces cut at successively lower levels remain as remnants on the valley walls. The lake bed sediments exposed on the valley floor and walls were subjected also to wind erosion, which lifted and carried the finer grades of sediment and deposited the material downwind, on the eastern side of the valley. Dunes formed on the bluff where the Smyth mansion was later situated.

The Neville terrace was cut at about 199 to 200 feet above sea level, some 60 feet below the highest lake beds. The river then swung away from the east wall, slipping to the right and westerly, as it continued to cut down. The surface of the terrace was weathered during this interval, as indicated by a 4 to 6 inch-deep zone of bright red-colored soil which was observed in an exposure still open in April 1970. Subsequently, the river returned to the east bank, perhaps by flooding, truncated the terrace by removing the topsoil and part of the red zone below it, and deposited a few inches of fluvial, clayey sand above the weathered lake beds. The elevation of this second terrace surface was probably about the same as the original one, give or take a few inches.

The river slipped away from the east bank again and, staying within its modern channel, cut down to bedrock to form the falls. It may never again have flowed at the level of the Neville terrace (C. Koteff, personal

communication). In its place, wind deposition of fine sediments transported from the exposed lake beds of the valley floor and walls began
to raise the surface of the terrace and continued to raise the surface of
the bluff above it.

Almost immediately after the river left the terrace for the second
time — before chemical weathering of the fluvial sediments had dis-
colored the yellow sand — people settled upon the surface and began to
deposit hearth debris, broken tools, and organic and lithic wastes. They
continued to live there, perhaps intermittently, for 8,000 years, while
aeolian deposition raised the terrace surface. The modern elevation of
205 feet reflects 5 feet of aeolian deposit and an upper foot of disturbed
overburden. The Neville terrace is now the first eastern terrace above
the modern floodplain; it is not known to be subject to flooding.

Sediment Analysis

In order to check the field interpretation of aeolian aggradation of the
terrace surface, a simple sediment study was undertaken. A soil monolith had been preserved by the excavators from the south face of
square N1E3. The monolith was 4 x 4 inches square, and included the
lowest 5 feet of the profile. Ten 100-gram samples were taken from the
monolith at 6-inch intervals, from the positions indicated on figure 6.
The samples were shaken for ten minutes each through a series of three
soil sieves of mesh sizes 10, 40, and 200. The material retained on the
sieves and that passing through the 200 mesh were weighed to the
nearest tenth of a gram. Cultural material on the 10 mesh screen was removed by hand before weighing, and the sample size was corrected for
subsequent calculations of percentages. The particle sizes in the four
fractions are given in table 1. The percentages by weight of the four
fractions for the ten samples are graphed in figure 5.

The four fractions thus separated are too gross to support much interpretation of the sedimentary history of the terrace. The small soil
sample available to us made the use of more sieve grades unfeasible,
and the uniqueness of the sample precluded any control comparisons
with other parts of the site. Detailed interpretation is precluded also by
the lack of data on past wind velocities, on the composition, distance,
and direction of the source material, and on past vegetation cover at
the source and on the terrace. For all these reasons, many interesting
questions which can be asked about the sedimentation history of the
Neville terrace cannot be answered.

It does seem reasonable to conclude, on the basis of the sediment
size composition described in figure 5 and table 1, that wind was the
major agent of deposition. The dominant C and D fractions of the deposit are composed of particles less than .42 mm in diameter. Such
particles are well within the size range of effective wind transportation,

TABLE 1

PARTICLE SIZES OF SEDIMENT FRACTIONS

Fraction	Mesh	Particle Grade	Particle Size
A	10	Pebbles to Very Coarse Sand	2.5mm - 2mm
B	40	Very Coarse Sand to Medium Sand	2mm - .42mm
C	200	Medium Sand to Very Fine Sand	.42mm - .074mm
D	passed 200	Very Fine Sand, Silt, and Clay	.074mm

even at gentle to moderate wind speeds. Particles less than .2 mm in diameter are small enough to be carried in suspension by winds and transported for great distances as dust (Garrels 1951, pp. 130-134). All of the D fraction and some of the C fraction particles are smaller than .2 mm. The reduction in the percentage of the D fraction above the level of the fluvial deposit (Sample 1) is indicative of the action of a sorting agent such as wind which, passing over the terrace and being slowed by the bluff, would deposit the coarsest fraction of its load (C) and carry the finest particles (D) farther downwind. The composition of Samples 2 through 10, with the dominance of the C fraction, is very suggestive of deposition by wind at a short distance from fine-grained source material. That source is assumed to be the glaciolacustrine beds and fine-grained river deposits which were abundant immediately to the west of the terrace.

The minor fractions A and B, which are comprised of the largest particles, are minimal in Sample 1; they increase significantly only in Samples 6 and 7. Interpretation of this pattern was difficult. We considered the possibility of an episode of flooding at the level of Samples 6 and 7, but could find no support for this hypothesis in the natural or cultural stratigraphy elsewhere on the site. There is no widespread erosional unconformity or sterile deposit at the site, one or both of which would be expected in the case of a flood. Upon the suggestion of Carl Koteff that a cultural explanation be sought, the A and B fractions of Samples 5, 6, and 7 were observed under a binocular microscope at 30X magnification. It was expected that the mineral grains would be rounded if their source was floodwater and that cultural debris — from stone boiling, rock chipping, etc. — would be angular. In fact, both rounded and angular mineral particles were observed. Samples 6 and 7 had high frequencies of rounded mineral fragments, with very little angular lithic debris. However, there was found to be a significant but unquantified amount of organic material in these samples, in the form of charcoal specks and comminuted calcined bone. The best interpretation at this stage of the inquiry seems to be that the coarse fractions A and B result from human activity at the site; they include some river sand, perhaps brought to the terrace for special task purposes. Further refinement of this analysis was not attempted because only the one soil monolith was available and there were, as a result, no experimental controls possible.

Paleoecology

The first samples taken from the soil monolith were a set selected for pollen analysis. The palynologist reported that no pollen grains were preserved in the light, oxidized soil of the site. Furthermore, no pollen sequences have been studied in the Manchester area. It is possible to make some general statements about past regional climates and vegetative cover, on the basis of studies made elsewhere in New England and the North Atlantic ocean. These extrinsic data will be cited in later chapters when they bear upon the cultural interpretations or conclusions.

Soil samples taken from features in the lowest stratum of the site were passed through fine sieves in the laboratory. No seeds or other macrobotanical remains except wood charcoal were present. It has not yet been possible to arrange for a study of the wood charcoal from the site, which might conceivably provide some paleoecological data. The difficulty of distinguishing between cultural and environmental constraints on the charcoal sample is great enough to diminish the appeal of such a study in the absence of control data from other sources.

Fauna was no better preserved than flora in the site's soil, which was mildly acidic. A test run for Peter McLane in 1968 at the University of New Hampshire's Agricultural Experiment Station at Durham determined a pH value of 6.0 for a soil sample taken 45 inches deep in square N3W1. The only bone preserved at all was scraps and minute fragments of calcined bone, none of which could be identified at even the genus level. Some of it is definitely mammalian, and some piscine. The A, B, and C fractions of the sediment samples contained fragments of calcined bone of the relevant sizes, including some articular portions of bones from very small mammals and small fish. The rich organic content of the soil was demonstrated by microchemical measurements of phosphorous. The results of this study will be discussed in chapter 3.

PHYSICAL STRATIGRAPHY

Excavation Methods and Records

At the beginning of the 1968 field season, two datum lines were laid out at the site to control the grid of five-foot squares. The north-south baseline was oriented parallel to the back wall of the Neville house and placed to bisect the back yard. The east-west datum line was perpendicular to the south end of the baseline, a short distance north of the embankment of West Salmon Street. Squares were numbered at five-foot intervals north along the baseline and both east and west of it (fig. 2). The ground surface was close to horizontal along the north-south base line, rising no more than 4 inches in 60 feet. Along the east-west line there was a slope down to the west. In the major excavation area, between N1 and N1E3, the slope was minimal. It rose to the east, so that the surface of square N1E9 was 41 inches higher than that of N1E3.

Excavation procedures were described by Peter McLane in the preliminary report he was drafting in 1969:

Arbitrary 3" levels for recovery and bagging of material were used. Lack of good definition of zone boundaries and extreme thickness of zones forced the use of artificial 3" levels for all digging. Because of manpower and time limitation as well as the salvage nature of the operation, troweling was used only for features or artifacts encountered. The 5 foot squares were taken down by quarter sections and ¼" to ½" depths using square edged shovels. It was felt that reasonably good control was maintained especially by using the shovel in reverse position with a dragging motion towards the digger. With practice this method can approach troweling in thinness of material removed and in sensitivity to echo sounds of artifacts struck, especially if the lightest weight thin blade shovel is used. All material was screened through 3 to-the-inch mesh wire.

Excavation records consisted mainly of notations and sketches on the faces of the paper bags which received the materials recovered from each 3-inch level. In addition, there were three scaled drawings of profiles prepared in the field, recording the north wall of N3W1, the west wall of N8, and the south wall of N1E9. Color photographs and slides recorded fourteen profiles, most of which included scales. Some sketches and photographs of floor plans and features were made. Inventory sheets for twenty-seven of the thirty-four squares had been prepared by the excavators, not all of which were complete. The soil monolith from the south face of square N1E3 was an invaluable record, whose usefulness was diminished only by its uniqueness.

At the Peabody Museum, between 1970 and 1972, records were compiled square by square. The bag notes were xeroxed for ease of handling and filed by square. Scaled profile drawings were prepared from projected photographic slides and from enlarged color prints. Soil and charcoal samples were cross-referenced. A feature catalogue was compiled. Flake counts and raw material frequencies were graphed for each square. As the analysis proceeded, the files for each square were

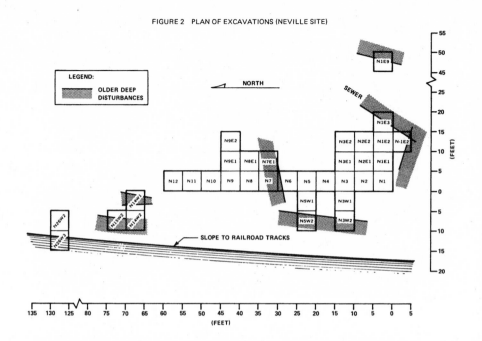

FIGURE 2   PLAN OF EXCAVATIONS (NEVILLE SITE)

augmented by artifact and feature stratigraphies. Maximal depths for ceramic recoveries were plotted as an adjunct to the feature records. By 1973, when the synthesis was begun, the individual records for each square were complete enough and consistent enough to inspire confidence.

Beginning his report in 1969, Peter McLane reflected with the wisdom of hindsight that "a relatively poor job of recording and note taking was done during excavations. This did not become really evident until the writing of this report." In fact, when all the records available for the present study were compiled and organized, a fair amount of detailed information was at hand. We miss the observations on soil color and texture which would have helped place stratigraphic unit interfaces more accurately. Feature recognition was minimal, and recording inconsistent, but those who saw the profiles *in situ* can understand and sympathize with the excavators' recognition problems. After working with the data for four years, I have confidence in the reliability of the records as far as they go.

Interpretation of the Stratigraphy

The excavators recognized four stratigraphic zones with cultural remains, which they encountered regularly but did not measure or record precisely in the field. The uppermost was a disturbed zone in which

Indian artifacts were intermingled with glass, ceramic, and metal objects of Anglo-American cultural origin. Below this was a zone of chocolate brown color extending from about 18 to 30 inches in depth. The thickest zone, called Black Indian dirt, extended to about 54 inches and was underlain in the southern squares by a lighter colored zone which was notable for its gray-silvery sheen. These zones were described and their approximate depths cited in McLane's preliminary report. They were mentioned only occasionally in the field notes.

I tested the original stratigraphic interpretation against the detailed data assembled between 1970 and 1973 and was able to define five strata, three of which were further subdivided. The major stratigraphic interfaces recognized in the second study correspond well with those reported by McLane. The definition of more than five distinct stratigraphic units instead of four has proven to be very helpful in the interpretation of the cultural sequence at the site.

The stratigraphic reinterpretation is based upon correspondences among several kinds of data, which were compiled independently and later found to be mutually supportive. Profiles for individual squares were prepared from field sketches and photographs. Stratigraphic interfaces were defined on the basis of excavators' observations as well as lensing and color phasing in photographs. No interfaces can be defined with less than an inherent 3-inch error because of the excavation and recording techniques. Within that margin of error, the interfaces are remarkably concordant. There is no doubt but that the strata throughout the excavated area were essentially horizontal and parallel to the modern surface.

Composite profiles were drawn for the north-south and east-west baselines; interfaces could be traced consistently between adjacent squares and could be matched by simple projection across 5- or 10-foot gaps where records were lacking. The north-south profile shown in figure 3 is a slightly simplified version of such a composite; the profiles of squares 4, 9, 12, and upper 5 are projected from adjacent recorded squares. Confidence engendered by the consistency of interface depths throughout the excavation led to the definition of a generalized stratigraphic column, which is used as the left-hand scale of the graphs in figures 8-13. The generalized, modal interface depths shown there coincide well with the artifact frequency peaks summarized for all squares, suggesting that most of the interfaces are major occupation floors. Such features as were recorded cluster close to or immediately below the modal interface depths. The major trend changes of the sediment fraction graph (fig. 5) occur at interfaces, as is shown by the dashed lines between samples on figure 4. The definition of five major strata, three of which are further subdivided, is based on the convergence of these several lines of inquiry. The strata were defined in total independence of the artifact typologies.

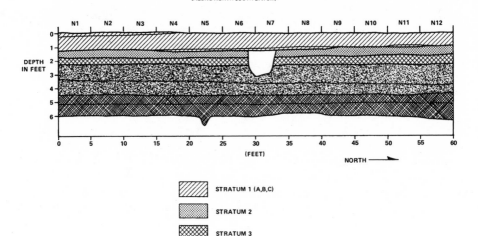

FIGURE 3   GENERALIZED STRATIGRAPHY
(ALONG NORTH-SOUTH DATUM)

STRATUM 1 (A,B,C)

STRATUM 2

STRATUM 3

STRATUM 4 (A,B)

STRATUM 5 (A,B)

Description of the Stratigraphy

In addition to the generalized stratigraphy shown on figures 3 and 8-13, specific profiles are illustrated on figures 4, 5, 7, and plate 1. Subdivisions of Strata 1, 4, and 5 are not visible in all examples. The strata and their subdivisions are described and interpreted below.

Stratum 5

Stratum 5B was deposited directly on the surface of the fluvial terrace sediments, at a normal depth of 69 inches below the 1968 sod. There is no indication of any chemical weathering of the fluvial deposits below the aeolian sediments. Alternating dark and light lenses shown on plate 2 below 72 inches in square N1E1 (Feature 22) may record cultural activities below Stratum 5B, but no observations of the excavators provide information about them. The 5B/A interface occurred normally at 60 inches, where there was a major occupation floor. The stratum color was usually recorded as silvery-gray, and the excavators reported a peculiar sheen to these sediments. This was probably a light-refraction phenomenon caused by parallel alignment of the platy clay minerals in deposit. The relatively high proportion of clay-sized grains in the

Plate 1. Stratigraphic profile, N10 North Wall. Small labels at 1-foot intervals.

A

B

Plate 2. Features: a. Feature 14, group of stones resting on Stratum 4B in N5 and N6; b. Feature 22, postmold in alluvium below Stratum 5B.

sediment at this depth has been demonstrated (fig. 5, Sample 2). Color
lensing was more obvious in this stratum than in those above because
of the lighter background color. The N3W1 profile (fig. 4) indicates two
distinct floors in Stratum 5B, one at the base and one in the middle.

Stratum 5A, between 60 and 54 inches, was generally darker in color
than 5B, but shared the silvery sheen, especially in the southern half of
the excavation. The top of Stratum 5A, near 54 inches, was frequently
noted in the excavation records because of the color change and the
presence of the sheen. The separation between 5A and 5B near 60 inches
was not always observed (fig. 4) but was consistent enough to make
the distinction worthwhile. It gains significance with the cultural stratigraphy to be discussed in chapter 3.

Stratum 5, A and B, is equivalent to Zone II of the preliminary report (Dincauze 1971). All four radiocarbon ages of the eighth millennium B.P. were calculated on samples from this stratum, in addition to
two younger ones (dates discussed in chapter 3). Stratum 5 accumulated over a period of at least seven radiocarbon centuries before 7,000
B.P. to a total thickness of about 15 inches.

Stratum 4

Stratum 4B extended from about 54 inches to 45 inches below the surface. In some squares, notably N10 and N2E2, the 5A/4B interface was
marked by a lens of lighter colored sediment. Otherwise, the contrast
with 5A was marked by the darker black of 4B. This was a typical
greasy, black midden soil, which included far less of the clay and silt
grade sediment fraction than did the stratum below it (fig. 5, Samples
4 and 5). The occupation floor at 45 inches has two associated radiocarbon ages (chapter 3) which average to 5985 B.P. With the age of the
5A/4B interface estimated at close to 7000 B.P., the 9 inches of Stratum 4B accumulated in about 1,000 radiocarbon years.

Stratum 4A extended from above the occupation floor at 45 inches
to the color change which marked the 4A/3 interface, between 27 and
30 inches below sod. Throughout its 15 inches of thickness, it was un-
differentiated black, greasy midden soil. The texture differed from that
of 4B in having larger proportions of the coarser sediment fractions (A
and especially B, figs. 5 and 6), which have been interpreted as cultural
introductions. Immediately above the 45-inch floor, a marked drop in
the frequency of artifacts was noted by all the excavators and confirmed by the artifact counts (figs. 8-13). No color change marked this
zone of low artifact frequency.

Stratum 4 is the equivalent of Zone III in the preliminary report.
Since 1971, the lower interface has been defined with greater clarity
and the distinctiveness of the A and B subdivisions has been recognized
and demonstrated.

Stratum 3

This is the same as Zone IV of the earlier report. Color change from
black to brown marked the interface between 4A and 3. It was gradual
and uneven, occurring normally between 30 and 27 inches deep, sometimes slightly deeper. The upper limit of the stratum was the irregular
base of the eighteenth-century plow zone, which reached 18 to 21
inches below the 1968 surface. The brown color of the stratum shows
up well in color photographs and slides and can be seen as tonal contrast on plate 1. The texture was similar to that of Stratum 4, with the
exception of an increase in the finest (D) fraction of sediment. Artifact
density was highest between 27 and 30 inches, where there was probably an occupation floor.

Artifacts younger than 3,500 years were present in Stratum 3 only
intrusively. It appears that the plow zone truncated the stratigraphy,
thoroughly mixing deposits less than 3,500 years old and creating Stratum 2. Strata 4A and 3 together accumulated between 6,000 and 3,500
radiocarbon years ago to a total depth of 24 inches.

Stratum 2

The excavators did not distinguish this lower plow zone from the later
overburden in recording their disturbed zone. The distinction was made
in the 1971 report, where the lower plow zone was called Zone V. This
stratum was normally about 9 inches thick from plow sole, which was
between 21 and 18 inches, to the overburden of Stratum 1, which began about 12 inches below the 1968 surface. A yellow lens of sediment,
sometimes gravelly and usually sterile of cultural debris, separated the
lower from the upper plow zone discontinuously over the excavated
area, at depths of 10 to 12 inches. Stratum 2 shows in the color photographs as a bleached tan zone, lighter than Stratum 3 and less gray than
most of Stratum 1. Sediment Sample 10 represents Stratum 2; its composition was close to that of Sample 8 from the 4A/3 interface indicating that Stratum 2 is a product of the same depositional processes as
the strata below it (fig. 5). Its structure was homogenized by the plowing, so no features or internal stratigraphy were preserved. This stratum
contained all the Woodland period prehistoric remains which were not
in pits, as well as seventeenth-, eighteenth-, and early nineteenth-century English and Anglo-American artifacts. The normal furrow direction observed in profiles was north-south paralleling the long axis of the
terrace. At the south end of the excavation, in the N2 row of squares,
there were a few east-west furrows below the north-south ones. Stratum
2 was buried by part of Stratum 1 in 1842. Nine inches of Stratum 2
accumulated in about 3,500 years. Nine inches is relatively thick for a

Colonial plow zone, so it does not seem that a great deal of sediment has been lost to erosion.

Stratum 1

This stratum, the upper 12 inches of deposit, includes a number of subsidiary layers superimposed on the 1842 surface which forms the 2/1 interface. It is the same as Zone VI of the preliminary report and corresponds to the upper two-thirds of the excavators' disturbed zone. In the southwest part of the excavated area, as many as four subdivisions (A through D) have been recognized within Stratum 1. The four subsidiary units observed in this stratum in the easternmost, isolated, square N1E9 may not be the same as A-D of the main area. They will not be further considered. Stratum 1B is the most widespread and thickest of the subdivisions. It is the superior plow zone, consisting of thoroughly mixed subsoil and other material containing nineteenth- and some twentieth-century cultural material as well as artifacts derived from underlying strata as deep as 5A. This overburden was probably derived from nearby railroad and road construction and the cellar hole excavation, all dating between 1835 and 1842. A culturally sterile, yellow lens, gravelly in places, underlies 1B discontinuously. It may be seen in figures 3 and 4, where it is indicated as 1C. Stratum 1D is localized, recorded only in N3W1 (fig. 4); it was a cinder lens, underlying 1C, which probably relates closely to the railroad construction of 1835-42. Above everything else, in the southwest area, lay 1A, a gravel lens thickening to the south and west. It is probably the tail of the embankment for West Salmon Street, deposited during reconstruction of the Amoskeag Bridge and its approach ramps in 1922.

FIGURE 4   SAMPLE PROFILES

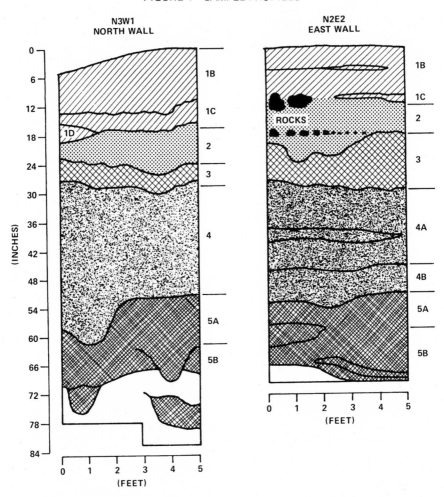

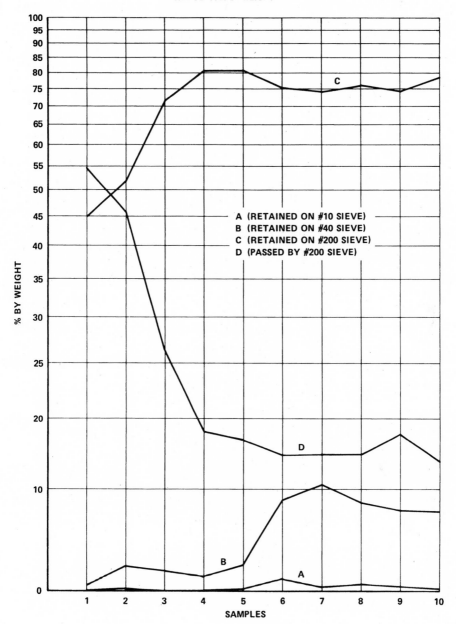

FIGURE 5   COMPOSITION OF SEDIMENT SAMPLES
SIZE CLASSES BY WEIGHT

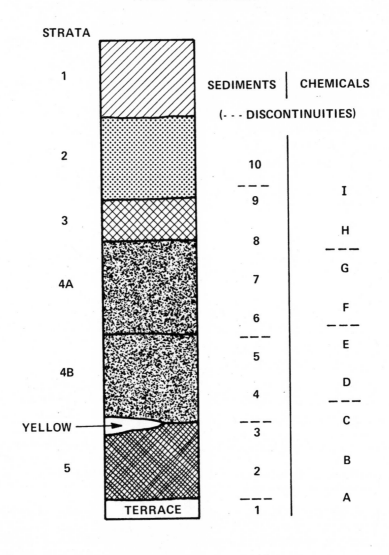

FIGURE 6   SOUTHWEST CORNER
N1E3 — SOIL COLUMN

2

Description of Artifacts and Features

From its inception, the artifact analysis was intended to be the main method for recognizing activity patterns at the site. For this purpose an attribute analysis is most suitable. The analysis has revealed many clusters of associated technical, morphological, stylistic, and functional attributes. Singly or in combination, the attributes inform about patterned behavior at the site, which was determined by both cultural traditions and task-specific behavior.

With the exceptions of unutilized flakes, fragments of large bifaces, and tip fragments of projectile points, all precolonial artifacts from the site were subjected to a detailed examination under a binocular microscope at magnifications betwen 10X and 30X. Attributes of form, manufacturing technique, and function were recorded for each artifact on individual record forms.

Classes of closely similar artifacts were isolated from the collection on the basis of shared sets of technical, morphological, and functional attributes. Technical attributes, representing the patterned behavior associated with manufacturing processes, were given primary consideration, instead of morphological-stylistic attributes. This procedure was chosen as a means of recognizing groups of artifacts which had been produced by similar sequences of patterned behavior. The products of such patterned behavior sequences are considered to be culturally equivalent artifacts — objects intended to serve similar or equivalent functions in a limited number of specific cultural contexts. The method is based upon the conviction that although ideal forms cannot be recognized among archaeological specimens, the products of patterned behavior can be recognized.

The artifacts available for study obviously constitute samples of larger populations. The samples were collected intensively from an arbitrarily limited area of a site of undefined dimensions. The size of the collection is large by New England standards (975 analyzed specimens), but few of the many artifact classes are quantitatively impressive.

The artifact classes described below will be considered as unbounded nodal clusters of attributes for some purposes, as equivalent to types for some other purposes. In the present study, the former concept will play the more important role. When Neville artifact classes are compared with artifacts from other sites and other collections, they may be most useful initially if considered as types. The types here presented are not, however, closely bounded by arbitrarily imposed definitive criteria; they are not defined so as to unequivocally include or exclude a given marginal specimen. Instead, internal variation is expressed in the class description. It is expected that artifacts separated in time or space from the populations of which these classes are samples will differ in their attribute distributions and associations, proportional to their chronological or spatial distance.

PROJECTILE POINTS

Neville Stemmed Points

Neville points are products of an ancient tradition of stemmed, stone projectile heads which was characteristic of the Archaic cultures of the Atlantic watershed of North America. Details of manufacturing techniques and morphology distinguish Neville points as a type from all other Eastern Archaic Stemmed points except for the Stanly Stemmed type of the Southeast (Coe 1964, p. 35). Only size (range and mean) distinguishes Neville from Stanly points, with the latter's means at the upper end of the Neville ranges. It is recognized that Neville points may logically be considered variants of the Stanly Stemmed type. The presence in the Northeast of projectile points related to the Stanly Stemmed type was not recognized until the excavation of the Neville site in 1968. Specimens like those here called Neville points have been referred to in Northeastern literature as "corner-removed" (Bullen 1949, p. 12, Pl. III 21, 22, 24), "corner-removed #5" (Fowler 1963, p. 3), and "hastate" (Ritchie 1969, pp. 144, 149).

Technology

Neville points were shaped from small bifaces or flakes bifacially modified. Flake preforms were recognized by some original scar surfaces and by occasional platform and bulb remnants at the bases of finished points. The preform was shaped by controlled percussion, which resulted in shallow expanding flake scars impinging on the midline. There is about an equal frequency of flake step-fracture and resolving at the midline. The cross sections are characteristically lenticular. Materials were fine-grained igneous rocks (56%), with minor representations of quartz (20%), argillites (17%), quartzites (4%), and chalcedony.

The haft element of stem and shoulder was defined by secondary percussion and pressure retouch after the initial shaping of the preform. The shoulder-to-stem angle was frequently (61%) defined by steep crushing retouch, probably by firm pressure against a tool or surface curved at the desired arc. The stem bases were thinned after the sides were shaped; the basal thinning was usually unifacial. The final step in manufacture was pressure retouch to regularize the blade edges. In contrast to the haft element retouch, which was usually continuous and bifacial, retouch on the blade was discontinuous. Regularity of blade outline was apparently more desirable than a sharp edge; blade edges were formed by both flat primary scars and deep, short, retouch scars. Only one specimen has serrated edges.

Morphology

A few Neville points from the type site are illustrated on plate 3. Their major dimensions are shown on table 2. The following mean ratios characterize the type population — L:W = 1.6:1, W:Th = 3.8:1, W:Shoulder Height (shape of haft element) = 2.8:1. The blades typically expand from the sharp tip to the shoulders, with straight (61%) or very slightly excurvate (24%) edges. Irregular and retouched blades complete the count. Unbroken tips of Neville points are sharp, acute, and carefully shaped. The shoulder angles, in spite of the wide range, tend to be less than 90° (61%).

The stems usually contract toward the base (71%); 20% of the stems have parallel edges, and 8% are slightly expanded. The stem bases are straight (31%), oblique (27%), concave (21%), convex (13%), or notched (8%). If slightly notched and concave bases are in fact one category, it is nearly as prevalent as straight bases (29%).

Function

The emphasis on careful shaping of the sharp tip and blade, as well as on the symmetry of the form, suggests that the intended function of these specimens was piercing. No edge wear indicative of a cutting, shaving, or scraping function was observed under 20X magnification. Roughly half of the specimens (52%) were broken across the blade, indicating considerable stress on that element of the tool. Stem breakage ran a poor second, with 18% affected; this pattern could result from breakage above a haft which extended partway up the face of the blade, supporting the stem and shoulder area. Five specimens (5%) had damaged tips; at least two of these were damaged by impact.

Temporal and Spatial Ranges

The stratigraphic distribution at the Neville site is shown in figure 9. Most of the specimens occurred in Stratum 5, A & B, with the peak fre-

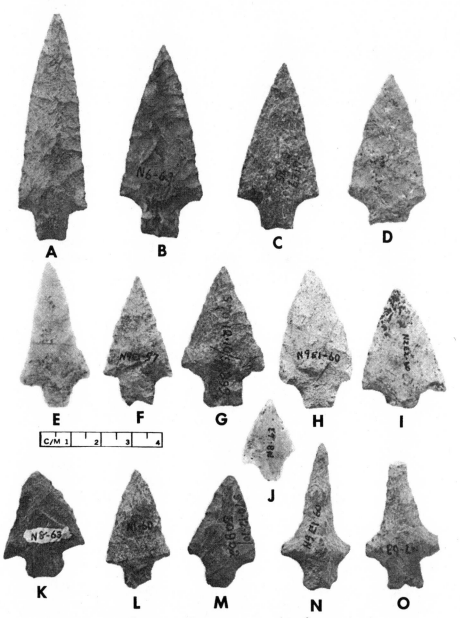

Plate 3. Neville Stemmed Points (a-m) and Perforators (n,o).

quency near the A/B interface. Neville points are the earliest type at the site. The radiocarbon dates for Stratum 5, ranging between 7015 and 7740 B.P., bracket the duration of Neville points there.

The spatial range of Neville points as presently recognized extends through New England from Connecticut to central Maine; they appear to become less frequent toward the northwest. Stanly Stemmed points conforming to the original definition in all respects are extremely rare in New England but have been reported at its southwestern margin on Staten Island (Ritchie and Funk 1971).

Neville Variants

Eleven projectile points with rounded stems display attributes which relate them to both the Neville and Stark types. They were lumped with Starks during preliminary sorting because of their obtuse shoulder angles and contracting stems. Once the technical analysis was done, they were seen to contrast sharply with the technical modes of the Stark type. All were made by Neville techniques, with the flat primary percussion flaking and discontinuous pressure retouch characteristic of that type. Five were made from flakes with the platform remnant at the base; two have crushed stem-to-shoulder angles. The blade cross sections are lenticular and the edges sharp. The raw materials were various felsites. Two of these points are illustrated on plate 6a, b. Their dimensions are given on table 2. A comparison of the tabled dimensions will reveal that the form of the haft elements of these specimens is closer to the Stark mode than to that of Neville points. The W:Shoulder Height ratio confirms this, being 1.7:1, the L:W ratio is 1.8:1, W:Th, 4:1.

Temporal and Spatial Ranges

There were not enough of these specimens to support any evaluation of their intermediate status. The stratigraphic relationships are ambiguous: five occurred in Stratum 5, between 57 and 66 inches; an additional three were in Stratum 4B; one in 4A; and 2 in Stratum 1, the nineteenth-century overburden. Thus, most of them were coeval with Stark points; they do not clearly precede the latter as transitional forms would be expected to do. There may be a functional reason for the adoption of the Stark hafting style by makers of Neville points.

In the classification used by the Massachusetts Archaeological Society, this point style is labeled "corner-removed #9" (Fowler 1963, p. 3). It has been reported in southeastern New England in association with Neville and Stark points at a number of sites.

Stark Stemmed Points

Stark projectile points are characterized by long narrow blades, tapered stems, and thick cross sections. They are homotaxial and apparently

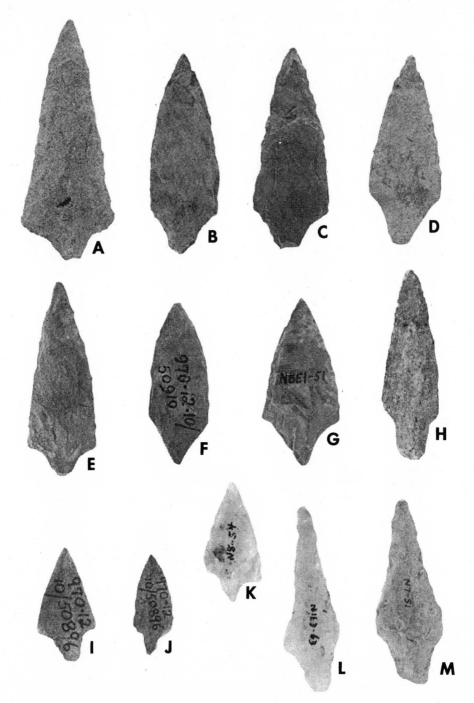

Plate 4. Stark Stemmed Points (a-k) and Perforators (l,m).

Plate 5. Merrimack Stemmed Points.

Plate 6. Bifaces from Stratum 5: a, b. Neville Variant point and fragment; d. Bifurcate-base point fragment; c, e, f. Fragments of large bifaces; g. Repaired perforator, simple shaft style.

coeval with the Morrow Mountain points of the Uwharrie sequence. Morphologically, at least, they closely resemble the Morrow Mountain

II style (Coe 1964, p. 37). Their nearest equivalent in the Northeast is the Poplar Island type of the Middle Atlantic region (Ritchie 1961, p. 44). In the classification of the Massachusetts Archaeological Society, Stark points are usually called "corner-removed #8" (Fowler 1963, p. 3). Small Stark specimens sometimes may be confused with Rossville points of the Early Woodland period (Ritchie 1961, p. 46, Plates 24, 26).

Technology

The blanks from which Stark points were made were often thick flakes or natural tabular slabs. Old blank surfaces are frequently visible on the faces of the finished specimens. While Stark makers were capable of competent bifacial percussion shaping (pl. 4a), they more often produced their projectile points by less refined methods. The points were shaped from the crude blanks by steeply angled, bifacial percussion flaking. The steep flakes often stepped or resolved well short of the midline. The flaking was continous around the entire periphery, without the change in directions or manner of flaking at the shoulder which characterized the production of Neville points. The discontinuous bifacial edge retouch on both blade and stem, probably pressure flaking, is usually steep and often overlapping, so that blunt, thick edges are typical. On many pieces it seems that edge strength, not sharpness, was desired. Sometimes the retouch is so steep and repetitious that the edges have a shattered look. Severe stem-edge grinding was observed on three specimens; a magnified view is illustrated on plate 22b. Sixty percent (60%) of the bases were thinned; 37% ended in a facet which was not obviously a platform remnant. Irregular and very thick cross sections are characteristic; this trait reflects both flaking technique and raw material selection. Stark makers often chose rocks which have poor flaking qualities, such as metamorphosed siltstones and tuffs (35%). They used various felsites (56%), especially rhyolite, quartz (7%) and unidentified stone (2%).

Morphology

Stark points are illustrated on plate 4; their dimensions are summarized on table 2. Mean ratios are L:W = 2:1, W:Th = 3:1, W:Shoulder Height = 1.4:1. The blade profiles are excurvate to the shoulder in 53% of the intact specimens; 33% have a straight expanding profile; and the remaining 14% are irregular. The shoulders are defined by obtuse angles. The majority of the specimens (83%) are symmetrical.

The stems taper toward the base in 96% of the sample; the remainder have parallel stem edges. Bases are typically pointed or sharply convex (75%). The remainder are straight, concave, or oblique in profile; some of these may have been broken.

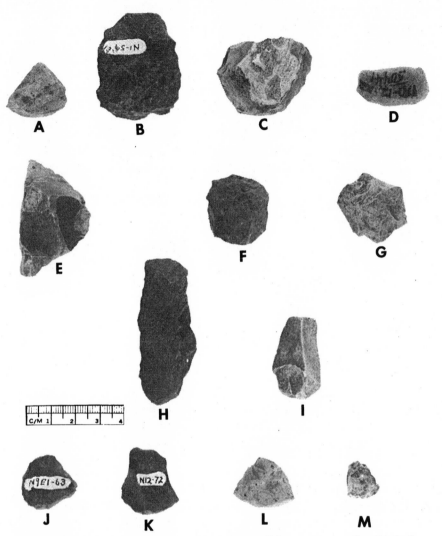

Plate 7. Middle Archaic Scrapers: a, b, c, d. Steep flake scrapers; e, f, g. Beaked scrapers; h, i. Carinated scrapers; j, k, l. Early flake end scrapers; m. Crystal scraper.

Function

Stark points, on the whole, are ill suited for any function but piercing. The narrow, thick blades with their sharp tips, blunted edges, and weak shoulders appear to be highly specialized piercers. The hafting mode is not obvious; the points could have been socket hafted. Almost half (46%) of the sample were broken across the blades, while 13% of the stems were broken, a pattern very close to that of the Neville points. No functional interpretation of the rounded shoulders, blunted edges, and tapered stems has been achieved, but one might be made in sites with faunal remains.

Temporal and Spatial Ranges

Stark points, as shown on figure 9, achieved their peak frequency later

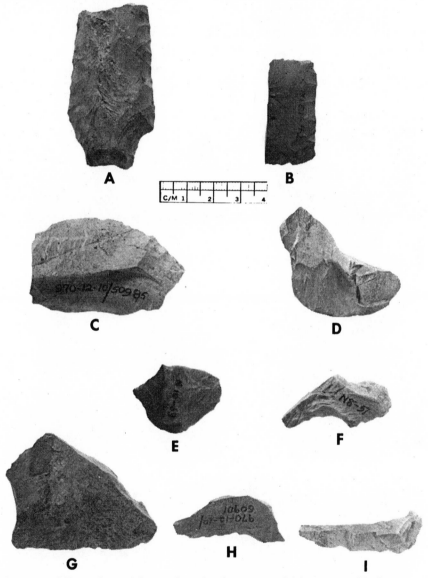

Plate 8. Middle Archaic Flake Tools and Bifaces: a. Kirk-like stemmed biface; b. Knife? fragment, biface; c, d. Flake knives (or side-scrapers); e. Backed flake knife of jasper; f. Spokeshave on core-rejuvenation flake; g. Flake knife; h. Flake knife or scraper; i. Flake knife.

than the Neville type, dominating at the Stratum 4B/5A interface. Their temporal position cannot be closely fixed, but probably cen-

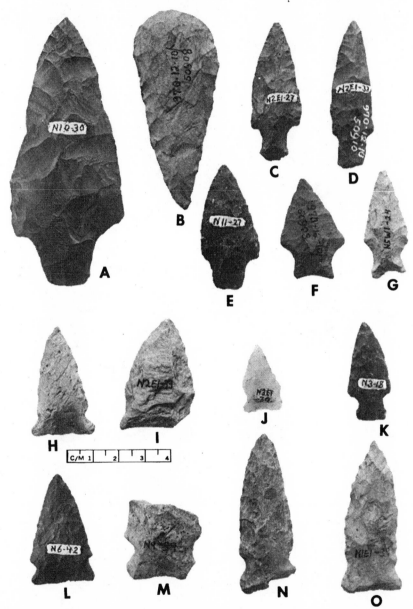

Plate 9. Late Archaic Projectile Points and Scraper: a. Atlantic implement blade; b. Large ovate biface scraper; c, d. Untyped stemmed points; e. Atlantic spearpoint; f. Wayland Notched point, Dudley variety; g. Orient point; h, i, o. Brewerton Eared-Notched points; j. Notched Triangular Point; k. Normanskill point; l. Vosburg point; m, n. Otter Creek points.

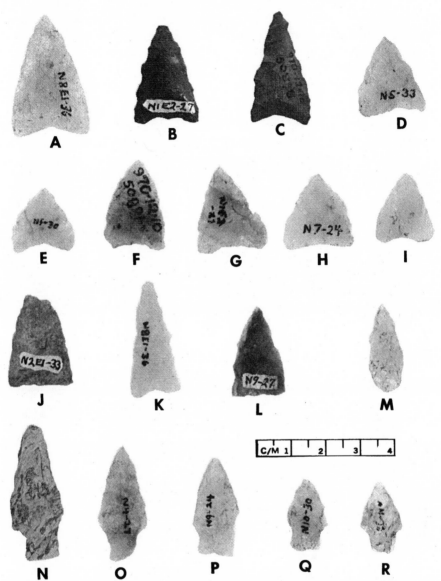

Plate 10. Late Archaic Triangles and Stemmed Points: a, d, e, f, g, h, i. Squibnocket Triangles; b, c, j, k, l. Beekman Triangles?; m. Squibnocket Stemmed point; n, o, p, q, r. Wading River points.

ters around 7000 B.P., extending an estimated 300 years in either direction.

The known distribution of Stark points is mainly southern and central New England, from Connecticut north to the Lake Winnipesaukee region of New Hampshire. They are more numerous than Neville points, being represented at more sites and often in higher numbers.

Merrimack Stemmed Points

The definition of Merrimack points is an advance toward resolution of the small stemmed point problem in the greater Northeast. They are older than all the small stemmed points of the Late Archaic and may

Plate 11. Small Stemmed II Points.

yet be demonstrated as the original of that stylistic series. Because
small stemmed points have rarely been described or carefully illus-

Plate 12. Woodland Projectile Points and Miscellaneous Bifaces: a, b. Levanna
points; c, d. Lanceolate bifaces; e. Lanceolate biface, cf. Greene point; f, g, h. Untyped stemmed points, cf. Lagoon; i. Lanceolate biface; j. Meadowood point; k, l.
Untyped side-notched points; m. Rossville point.

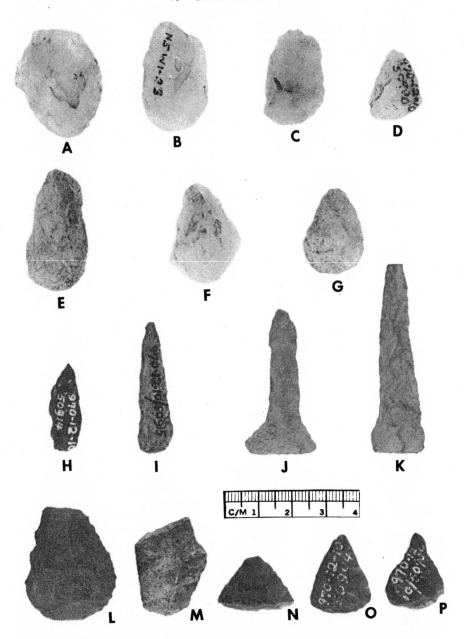

Plate 13. Late Archaic and Woodland Scrapers and Perforators: a, b, c, d. Biface scrapers; e, f, g. Expanded-bit scrapers; h. Reamer, simple shaft; i, k. Perforators, biface bases; j. Perforator, projectile point base; l, n. Flake scrapers; m. Long flake end scraper; o. Meadowood scraper; p. Perforator on Meadowood scraper.

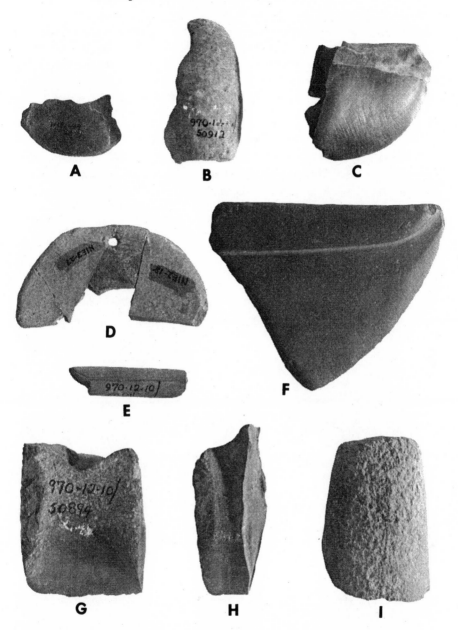

Plate 14. Ground Stone Tools: a. Spall knife; b. Ovoid atlatl weight; c. Half of Stanly type atlatl weight; d. Ground slate pendant; e. Ground slate fragment, possible hone; f. Semilunar knife fragment; g. Gouge bit, from Stratum 4A; h. Gouge fragment; i. Poll of ground stone tool.

trated in Northeastern reports, comparative statements are difficult to make. The Merrimack type does not seem to be represented anywhere in Fowler's 1963 classification of southern New England projectile points. The only comparable class presently in the literature is the original definition of the Bare Island point (Kinsey in Ritchie 1961, pp. 14-15). Merrimack points correspond closely to the description given there; and of the illustrated specimens on plate 2, numbers 11-15 are particularly good matches. More recent references to Bare Island points by Kinsey (1972, p. 123) and Funk (1965, p. 152) indicate that the definition of that type has been informally modified toward reference to Late Archaic stemmed points of quartz, like the Wading River type. None of the Merrimack points, however, are made of quartz, and none is of Late Archaic age.

Plate 15. Full-grooved Axe and Axe Preform: a. Axe with use-damaged bit; b. Preform, flaked and pecked.

Technology

The technical attributes of Merrimack points are close to those of Starks. Blanks were often flakes or naturally tabular slabs. The primary flaking was steeply angled, possibly performed with a hard hammer. Discontinuous bifacial retouch around the periphery stressed regularity of form over edge sharpness and often resulted in thick edges scarred by repeated step-fractures. Cross sections are thick, usually lenticular;

Plate 16. Pebble Tools and Core Hammer: a. Quartz core hammer; b, c. Pebble hammers; d. Notched pebble; e. Full-grooved pebble.

Plate 17. Choppers and Abrader: a. Picklike chopper; b. Chopper; c. Tabular abrader.

less often the sections are irregular, because of extreme step-fracture, or are thick triangles, reflecting the flake blank. Tips were carefully shaped on the long axis. Shoulders are small but well shaped.

The stems are bifacially flaked, and the bases thinned with precision. The stems are standardized in shape and size. Edge grinding, illustrated on plate 22c and d, occurs on all but one Merrimack stem. Three bases have a facet on one corner which may reflect an oblique orientation of the flake blank. The trait cluster of the stems is so consistent that the type may be recognized in a stem fragment. There is minimal overlap with the trait cluster of Neville stems, which are thinner, show basal flake orientation, and are essentially never ground.

The favored raw materials were fine-grained igneous rocks and quartzites. No specimens were made of quartz. Some argillites and metamorphosed tuffs, such as the Stark makers favored, were utilized also.

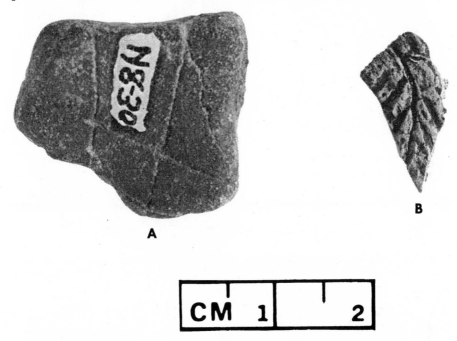

Plate 18. Engraved Pebble and Bone Fragment: a. Engraved arkose pebble; b. engraved bone, calcined.

Morphology

Merrimack points are small to medium-sized stemmed points with isosceles triangular blades, small shoulders, and nearly square stems. Some are illustrated on plate 5; their dimensions are summarized on table 2. Their mean ratios are L:W = 2.3:1, W:Th = 2.4:1, W:Shoulder Height = 1:1. The blades are mildly convex from the sharp tip to the shoulders, with 95% of the specimens exhibiting this trait. The only exceptions are

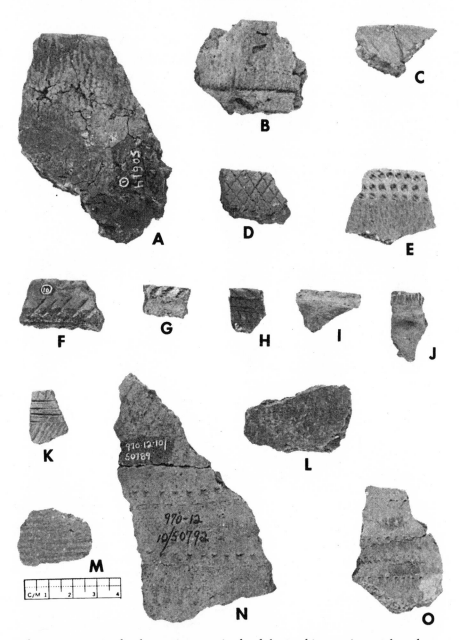

Plate 19. Ceramic Sherds: a. Vinette I rimsherd; b. Cord impressions and cord-wrapped stick, shell temper; c. Broad incisions, coarse grit temper; d. Criss-cross shell edge impressions, shell rocker-stamped interior; e. Corded punctations on incipient collar; f. Incision on neck and everted lip; g. Cord-wrapped stick, narrow collar; h. Fine incision on narrow collar; i. Undecorated narrow collar; j. Combed collar; k. Possible Chance Incised collar fragment; l. Bodysherd with fabric or basket impression; m. Corded body sherd, mica temper; n. Rocker-stamped and incised sherd from Feature 41; o. Rocker-stamped body sherd.

Plate 20. Artifacts from Feature 41: a. Rocker-stamped body sherd (cf. pl. 19n); b. Corner-notched point.

straight edges. The small, neatly delineated shoulders are obtuse angled (76%) or rounded (24%).

The stems are parallel sided (72%), slightly expanded (18%), or slightly contracted (10%). The bases are straight (85%) or mildly convex (14%), never concave.

Function

Merrimack points, with their stout, dull blades, sharp tips, and standardized haft elements, were made to be firmly hafted, piercing implements, which saw heavy use. Twice as many specimens broke just below the shoulder as above, and about one-third of the extant blades have damaged tips. A lashed hafting would almost surely be as wide as the shoulder, so that the weapon was unbarbed, perhaps intended to be easily withdrawn after piercing.

Temporal and Spatial Ranges

The stratigraphy is summarized in figure 9. Merrimack points dominate Stratum 4B, occurring on and below the floor at the 4A/4B interface which is dated to 5910 and 6060 B.P. The considerable overlap with the latter half of the Stark temporal range may reflect historical reality. Merrimacks do not appear to be coeval with Neville points; the small overlap in stratigraphy is almost certainly due to disturbance, as discussed in chapter 3.

The spatial distribution of Merrimack points is presently unknown. They seem to be rare elsewhere in New England, and they are represented in only a few collections from the Greater Boston area and from

Plate 21. Rocker-Stamped Vessel: Partial Reconstruction.

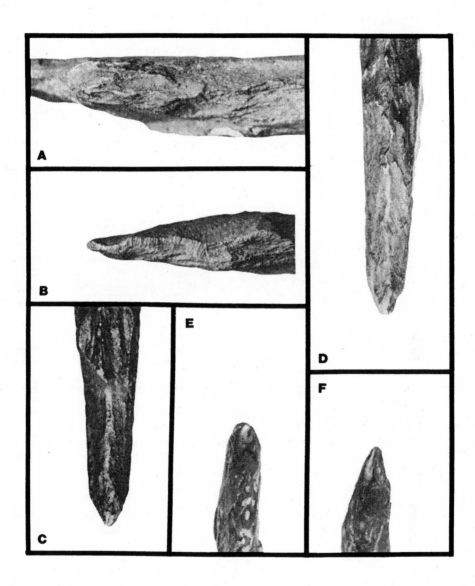

Plate 22. a. Stark Point: Shoulder Wear (pl. 4c); b. Stark Point: Stem Edge Grinding (pl. 4f); c. Merrimack Point: Stem Edge Grinding, Extreme (pl. 5a); d. Merrimack Point: Stem Edge Grinding, Normal (pl. 5a); e. Worn Tip of Perforator (pl. 13p); f. Worn Tip of Perforator: Reamer (pl. 13h).

the Shawsheen River area of northeastern Massachusetts surveyed by Bullen (1949, pl. III, 12).

Vosburg and Related Points

One unequivocal Vosburg point, made of black chert, was recovered near the base of Stratum 4A (Ritchie 1961, p. 55). It is illustrated on plate 9l. At the same level, in other squares, two corner-notched basal fragments of felsite were found. The basal dimensions and shape of all three specimens are closely comparable. The chert point was shaped by pressure flaking; the felsite pieces were percussion flaked.

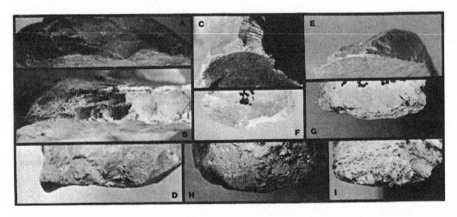

Plate 23. a. Resharpened Worn Edge: Steep Flake Scraper (pl. 7b); b. Edge Wear: Steep Flake Scraper (pl. 7c); c. Edge Wear: Beaked Scraper (pl. 7e); d. Edge Flaking: Beaked Scraper (pl. 7f); e. Edge Wear: Carinated Scraper (pl. 7h); f. Edge of Crystal Scraper (pl. 7m); g. Edge of Biface Scraper (pl. 13d); h. Edge of Expanded-bit Scraper (pl. 13e); i. Edge of Long Flake End Scraper (pl. 13m).

TABLE 2

DIMENSIONS OF PROJECTILE POINTS

	RANGE		MEAN	s	n
1. NEVILLE TYPE					
Length	2.30 -	6.30	3.77	0.86	33
Max. Width	1.65 -	3.25	2.40	0.30	72
Ht. Max. Width	0.30 -	1.75	0.86	0.49	69
Width Base	0.45 -	1.50	0.69	0.24	79
Stem. Min.	0.45 -	1.35	0.69	0.28	79
Max. Thick.	0.30 -	1.00	0.63	0.14	75
Edge $\angle$	35.00° -	75.00°	56.52°	8.59	74
Shoulder $\angle$	52.00° -	123.00°	86.52°	14.44	121
2. NEVILLE VARIANT					
Length	3.40 -	5.75	4.57	1.17	2
Max. Width	1.90 -	3.00	2.53	0.31	10
Ht. Max. Width	0.90 -	2.20	1.47	0.50	10
Width Base	0.50 -	1.15	0.71	0.20	8
Stem. Min.	0.50 -	1.15	0.71	0.20	8
Max. Thick.	0.50 -	0.85	0.63	0.10	10
Edge $\angle$	38.00° -	56.00°	46.50°	7.27	9
Shoulder $\angle$	82.00° -	127.00°	108.40°	13.53	17
3. STARK TYPE					
Length	2.90 -	6.90	4.29	1.00	25
Max. Width	1.20 -	3.05	2.12	0.36	53
Ht. Max. Width	0.80 -	3.00	1.48	0.44	54
Width Base	0.25 -	0.90	0.59	0.18	32
Stem. Min.	0.25 -	0.90	0.59	0.18	32
Max. Thick.	0.30 -	1.02	0.70	0.15	54
Edge $\angle$	35.00° -	85.00°	63.22°	9.16	53
Shoulder $\angle$	70.00° -	148.00°	115.29°	15.66	91
4. MERRIMACK TYPE					
Length	2.70 -	5.75	3.92	0.81	13
Max. Width	1.45 -	2.00	1.71	0.13	34
Ht. Max Width	1.15 -	2.35	1.64	0.28	33
Width Base	0.75 -	1.90	1.23	0.19	59
Stem. Min.	0.75 -	1.90	1.21	0.19	59
Max. Thick.	0.50 -	0.87	0.70	0.09	28
Edge $\angle$	53.00° -	85.00°	65.96°	6.97	30
Shoulder $\angle$	99.00° -	148.00°	133.28°	9.90	49

Table 2

		RANGE		MEAN	s	n
5.	WADING RIVER TYPE					
	Length	2.10	- 3.90	3.00	0.51	7
	Max. Width	1.20	- 1.80	1.46	0.17	13
	Ht. Max. Width	0.85	- 1.85	1.23	0.27	13
	Width Base	0.47	- 1.50	0.86	0.23	14
	Stem. Min.	0.47	- 1.50	0.85	0.23	13
	Width Below Sh.	0.80	- 1.20	1.00	0.11	8
	Max. Thick.	0.35	- 0.90	0.59	0.16	13
	Edge $\angle$	53.00°	- 80.00°	63.33°	10.03	9
	Shoulder $\angle$	98.00°	- 150.00°	125.45°	11.36	24
6.	SMALL STEMMED II					
	Length	1.95	- 4.15	2.93	0.52	33
	Max. Width	1.05	- 1.70	1.33	0.16	34
	Ht. Max. Width	0.90	- 2.30	1.40	0.29	33
	Width Base	0.25	- 0.80	0.50	0.13	30
	Stem. Min.	0.25	- 0.80	0.50	0.13	30
	Width Below Sh.	0.70	- 1.20	0.96	0.14	33
	Max. Thick	0.32	- 1.00	0.65	0.15	34
	Edge $\angle$	46.00°	- 87.00°	67.53°	10.40	30
	Shoulder $\angle$	113.00°	- 153.00°	132.11°	8.73	42

Wading River Points

These Late Archaic small stemmed points are difficult to identify with
confidence because of great latitude in the published definition (Ritchie
1969b, p. 241). The specimens here called Wading River are fifteen in
number, of which five are illustrated on plate 10n-r. The dimensions are
displayed on table 2. Mean ratios are L:W = 2:1, W:Th = 2.4:1,
W:Shoulder Height = 1.2:1. This series has been selected out of a far
greater number of small stemmed points on the basis of their squarish
stems, triangular blades, and crisp shoulders, by comparison with published illustrations (Ritchie 1959, 1969b) rather than by reliance on the
type definition. No great importance is attached to the composition of
this group. On figure 10, their stratigraphic distribution is shown to extend from the upper part of Stratum 4A into Stratum 3, where they at-
tain their highest frequency. Because the identification is uncertain and
the numbers small, no conclusions should be drawn from the fact that
they peak above the maximum frequency of the small stemmed II
group. The points called Wading River are made of quartz (60%), felsites
(27%), and miscellaneous materials.

Small Stemmed II Points

This grouping emerged during the analysis of the large series of small stemmed points from the Neville site. Its boundaries are defined by morphological attributes only; no cluster of technological attributes could be demonstrated. Because of the latter failure, this group will not be defined as a type. It is adopted here as a convenience for description only. Few if any of the specimens in the group conform to the Wading River or Squibnocket Stemmed types of Ritchie (1969b), nor are they equivalent to any of Fowler's small stemmed subclasses (1963, p. 3).

Technology

The wide variation in technological attributes may be related to, if not explained by, the fact that most of these points were made of quartz or quartzite (70%). The remainder are of felsite and argillite. Cross sections are thick, 45% biconvex and 55% plano-convex to irregular. Primary flaking and retouch were either bifacial or unifacial, with no necessary consistency on individual specimens. It is difficult to be certain, but both percussion and pressure flaking appear to have been used as primary shaping techniques. Within the group, approximately equal numbers of trimmed and untrimmed bases are represented, showing no consistent association with other traits.

Morphology

Selected specimens are illustrated on plate 11; their dimensions are summarized on table 2. The group is characterized by obtuse angle shoulders which form a gradual transition between excurvate blade and contracting stem. The great majority of the points are symmetrical and most have sharp tips. The stems contract toward convex or pointed bases. Ratios are L:W = 2.2:1, W:Th = 2:1, and W:Shoulder Height = .95:1.

Function

The standardization of major dimensions within this group, particularly those dimensions below the shoulder, is notable. The specimens, however made, could have been used interchangeably in socket hafts. They may have been parts of dart foreshafts. The special difficulties of dealing with fragments of quartz artifacts prevented consideration of breakage patterns for this group.

Temporal and Spatial Ranges

Figure 10 shows small stemmed II points continuously distributed from Stratum 4A through Stratum 3. They are Late Archaic points and possibly belong fairly early in that period. The two deepest specimens are from the same square and may have been intrusive at that depth.

This shape is not characteristic of points from southern New England

Late Archaic sites. It is not illustrated by Ritchie for Long Island (1959) or Martha's Vineyard (1969b), nor by Fowler for sites in Rhode Island or southeastern Massachusetts. I have met it before at the Atlantic Ledges site in Hull (Dincauze 1972, Plate VII 12). It may, therefore, be at home in central New England, as a regional variant of the small stemmed idea, related to the Wading River, Squibnocket Stemmed, and Lamoka types to the south and west.

Squibnocket and Beekman Triangles

Tentatively, a distinction between Squibnocket and Beekman Triangles has been made on the basis of published descriptions (Ritchie 1969b, p. 244; Funk in Ritchie 1971, p. 121), identifying Squibnockets by concave bases and rounded corners and Beekmans by straighter bases, crisper corners, and narrower proportions. They are illustrated together on plate 10a-l, where the contrasts may be seen to be minimal. Only the Squibnocket Triangles were plotted on the stratigraphic chart, figure 10. There were too few Beekmans to plot separately; had the types been combined on the graph, the peak would remain in the same place, near the Stratum 3/4A interface, but would be exaggerated, surpassing that of the small stemmed points and occurring slightly later. Stratigrapically, the only distinction between the two types is that no Beekman forms were found above the 27-inch level. Of the total sample of thirty-two typed Late Archaic triangles, 68% were identified as Squibnockets. Quartz is the dominant raw material (84%), with felsites the only other choice.

Among a number of other broken or unique small triangular bifaces in Strata 3 and 4A, three small notched triangles from 4A deserve mention. They were found in the 30-, 33-, and 36-inch levels; two were recovered from a single square. One is illustrated on plate 9j.

PERFORATORS

Bifacially flaked narrow perforator shafts were recovered from all strata except Stratum 1. Their frequencies parallel total artifact frequencies except for a drop near the 3/4A interface (fig. 13).

Morphology, Technology, and Provenience

No technological subdivisions of the perforator class could be distinguished, except choice of blank, so that perforators will be discussed by morphological categories only. Forty percent (40%) of the sixty-one specimens in the collection were tip and shaft fragments which cannot be sorted by morphological criteria. Among the 60% of specimens with formal attributes there are four obvious morphological classes: simple shafts, shafts on flakes, shafts on bifaces with irregular expanded bases, and shafts with projectile point bases.

Simple shafts (15%) are essentially restricted to Stratum 5, where all but two were recovered. An extraordinary quartzite specimen of this class is illustrated on plate 6g.

Perforator shafts on flakes are uncommon in this collection, amounting to only 8% of the total. They occurred in Strata 3, 4A, and 5A.

Perforator shafts on unspecialized bifaces account for 18% of the collection. They are unevenly distributed, four coming from Stratum 2, three from Stratum 5 at the A/B interface, and only one each from Strata 3 and 4. Specimens without provenience complete the count.

Perforators with projectile point bases (19%) are most characteristic of the Middle Archaic and the latter part of the Late Archaic zones. Both Neville and Stark type bases can be recognized on Middle Archaic perforators (pls. 3n, o and 4l, m), and at least one Late Archaic perforator has a Wayland Notched base (pl. 13j; Dincauze 1968, pp. 23-24).

Function

Very few specimens preserved wear marks. Two heavily worn specimens are therefore atypical. One is a perforator shaft worked on a bifacial scraper, probably from a Meadowood context. It is illustrated on plate 13p; a close-up view of the tip, worn by rotary motion, is given on plate 22e. The second heavily worn specimen, illustrated on plates 13h and 22f, was also used with a rotary motion, as striations on the faceted edges indicate. The span between the worn facets is close to the modal dimension below the shoulders of small stemmed points; this tool could have been used to ream sockets for hafting those points. Its recovery from the Strata 3/4A interface is consistent with such use. Otherwise, there are two major wear patterns: damaged tips and worn edges. They do not occur together on the same pieces. Tip damage shows no clustering in the stratigraphy. Edge damage, except for the two extreme examples described above, occurs only in the Middle Archaic Strata 4B and 5. The long shaft perforator on plate 6g is a typical example; it had broken with a transverse snap just below a zone of edge-wear 1 cm below the tip. The repaired piece shows that some rechipping had been done after the breakage.

SCRAPERS

Twelve types of small tools with various scraper functions were defined. They all have restricted stratigraphic ranges. Eight of the types are unifacial tools; the four bifacial types were found only in the upper strata — 2, 3, and 4A.

Steep-bitted Flake Scrapers

Technology

Steep flake scrapers were shaped on flakes selected for thickness exceeding .7 cm. The working edges were formed by steep flaking, probably percussion, at angles averaging 73° (see table 3 for details). On six specimens, a small projecting nose was worked somewhere on the edge. Resharpening flakes usually ended in step-fractures. None of the scrapers has a prepared haft element. The choice of quartz flakes for 47% of the sample probably reflects the relative frequency of thick flakes in that material. The next most frequent material class, 28%, was a variety of felsites. Argillites, quartzites, and miscellaneous materials together amount to 25%, in that order.

Morphology

These scrapers have a convex working edge, which tends to be sinuous rather than regular in outline. The few intact specimens approach a square or circular outline, with L:W ratios of 1:1. Four specimens are illustrated on plate 7a-d; dimensions are summarized on table 3.

Function

The steep bit angle of these scrapers is a suitable shape for heavy use (Wilmsen 1968, p. 159), and the observable wear suggests such employment. The bits are often (47%) crushed toward the dorsal surface, indicating that the tool was used on edge, with the ventral surface leading, under considerable pressure against a hard or tough surface. On specimens with noses, the protrusions received the heaviest wear. Hard use and heavy pressure is also indicated by the breakage pattern. The scrapers snapped under strain, the breaks appearing as chords across the bit arcs. On a few specimens there were two such breaks, probably sequential, the second terminating the useful life of the tool.

A minority wear pattern was observed only on three felsite specimens. On these the bit edges were worn smooth, in the typical endscraper pattern indicative of use on yielding gritty surfaces such as hides (pl. 23a, b). Two of these lay near the 4B/5A interface.

The major function of steep-bitted flake scrapers therefore appears to have been in working hard wood or bone.

Temporal and Spatial Distribution

All but one member of this class (96%) were recovered from below the Stratum 4A/4B interface, in the Middle Archaic levels of the site. They cluster significantly near the interfaces of 4B, 5A, and 5B, as shown on figure 12. They were most numerous south of the N5 row of squares (75%), becoming less frequent toward the north.

With scrapers receiving scant attention in the Northeastern literature, it is difficult to make comparative statements. The Large Beaked Flake Scrapers at the Wells Creek Crater site appear to be similar, although much larger, tools (Dragoo 1973, p. 37). Artifacts as technically crude and as heavily damaged as these may be easily overlooked. However, the evidence at the Neville site indicates that steep-bitted flake scrapers may be diagnostic of Middle Archaic occupations in the Northeast.

Quartz Crystal Scrapers

Four small unifacial artifacts of quartz crystal from Stratum 5 are described here because of their formal resemblance to flake end scrapers.

Technology

They are flake tools with secondary unifacial trimming on the end and sides. Generally, the broad end has the steepest edge. One specimen has a crushed edge, like that of scrapers used on hard material. The other three have a spalled edge, possibly broken under strain. An attempt has been made to illustrate a spalled edge on plate 23f.

Morphology

All are similar in size, ranging from 1.5 to 1.9 cm in length, 1.4 to 1.6 cm in maximum width, and .5 to .7 cm in maximum thickness. One is illustrated on plate 7m.

Function

It has not been possible to determine whether such implements were actually used as scrapers.

Temporal and Spatial Distribution

These all occurred in Stratum 5 on the southern end of the site, in squares N2E1, N3E1, and N-1E2. In N2E1, two specimens were in adjacent levels at the 5A/5B interface.

Beaked Scrapers

Technology

Irregular, thick chunks of rock, which permitted the easy shaping from a plane surface of a steep, stout beak, were chosen from among waste flakes at the site. The beaks were formed by localized scraperlike unifacial chipping. The predominant material was felsite (81%), with quartz the only significant alternative (12%).

Morphology

The consistent characteristic of the type is a stout, beaklike unifacial protrusion, which usually shows signs of heavy use. Sixteen of these artifacts were recognized, of which four had two beaks. The dimensions of beaks on fifteen specimens are summarized on table 3, where a bimodal distribution of edge angles on the beaks is documented. Three specimens with two beaks have one of each edge angle class. The general shapelessness of these artifacts precludes further description and almost defies photography; three of them are illustrated on plate 7e-g.

Function

Use damage is observable on ten specimens, most of which have crushed bit edges (pl. 23c). Surface areas on the body, opposite the plane surface of the beaks, are worn smooth in three instances, indicating their function as bearing surfaces when pressure was applied to the beak. Use of the beaks against fairly hard material is indicated. The beaks could have served as tools to gouge or scrape shallow grooves in wood, bone, or antler, a use consistent with their form and wear patterns. The pairing of beaks with dissimilar edge angles on three specimens may have a functional significance.

Temporal and Spatial Distribution

As displayed on figure 12, 73% of beaked scrapers came from Strata 4B and 5, the Middle Archaic levels. The few specimens from above the 4A/4B interface may have been displaced by pitting from higher levels.

No exactly comparable specimens are known to me. Dragoo's Core Beaked Tools and Tabular Core Beaked Tools at Wells Creek Crater are similar in form (Dragoo 1973, p. 43). The Neville specimens are much smaller and are not shaped on true cores. However, beaked scrapers may be expressions of an ancient and durable technical tradition in the East.

Carinated Scrapers

Technology

This special class of flake end scrapers is characterized by bit trimming flakes converging toward a distinct ridge on the dorsal surface. They were made on flake blanks selected for their pronounced dorsal ridges. The blanks were not preshaped; some are cortical flakes; one is a platform rejuvenation flake. The converging flaking from the convex bit was done with a degree of care and precision not otherwise manifested on the tools.

Morphology

The dorsal ridge is best seen on plate 7i, although it is partly obscured by subsequent damage. The ridge is medial on five of the six specimens, the exception being illustrated in plate 7h. The specimens are irregular in form except for the carefully shaped bit; for this reason, only bit dimensions are shown on table 3. Lengths range from 3.4 to 6.1 cm, maximum widths from 1.9 to 2.9 cm; L:W ratios range from 3:2 to 3:1.

Function

Use-wear is of the end-scraper type, shown on plate 23e.

Temporal and Spatial Distribution

Four were in Stratum 4B (fig. 12), where they were associated with Merrimack points. Two specimens in the upper plow zones are probably displaced.

Keeled scrapers at the Plenge site in New Jersey are comparable in form and technique (Kraft 1973, pp. 95, 96). They are assumed to be part of the Paleo-Indian component there, but there is no possibility of stratigraphic confirmation.

Thick End Scrapers

Technology

End-scraper bits were shaped on selected thick flakes at angles ranging from 70° to 80°. No hafting modification was made.

Morphology

This is a small class of five end scrapers with shallowly convex bits. They range in length from 2.1 to 4.4 cm, in width from 1.9 to 3.2 cm. Maximal thickness is close to 1 cm, occuring near the bit. Otherwise, the forms are unstandardized.

Function

This class of scrapers is distinguished by the only instances of use-scars on the ventral surfaces. Three of the five specimens have such scars, indicating that the tool was used like a plane, with the dorsal surface uppermost.

Temporal and Spatial Distribution

Three of the five were found in the middle of Stratum 4B, at 48 inches. The other two were at the 4B/5A interface. There is some evidence for spatial clustering, in that two were in adjacent squares at 48 inches and two were within 6 inches of vertical distance in a single square. The clusters were widely separated on the north-south axis of the excavation.

Early Flake End Scrapers

Three small flake end scrapers from Stratum 5B, illustrated on plate 7j-l, are unlike any others in the Middle Archaic levels and deserve mention.

Technology

These specimens have scraper bits shaped by careful pressure flaking at the distal end of small flakes. No other retouch occurs; the sharp corners of specimens k and l on plate 7 are not graver spurs. The materials are unique at the site: chert for plate 7j, a volcanic stone which may be recrystallized obsidian for k, and a fine-grained lavender color felsite for l.

Morphology

They are smaller than all others at the site except for the quartz crystal scrapers and one from Stratum 2. None exceeds 3 cm in any dimension, and maximal thickness ranges only from .5 to .6 cm.

TABLE 3

DIMENSIONS OF SCRAPERS

MIDDLE ARCHAIC SCRAPERS

		RANGE			MEAN	n
1.	STEEP FLAKE SCRAPERS					
	Length	1.30	-	4.30	2.69 cm	16
	Width	1.70	-	4.00	2.70 cm	16
	Max. Thick.	.70	-	2.10	1.12 cm	27
	Bit Thick.	.50	-	1.30	0.72 cm	28
	Bit $\angle$	$55.00°$	-	$90.00°$	$73.20°$	35
2.	BEAKED SCRAPERS					
	Beak Width	.50	-	1.90	1.08 cm	19
	Beak Convexity	.30	-	.60	.44 cm	19
	Bit $\angle > 75°$	$85.00°$	-	$90.00°$	$88.00°$	5
	Bit $\angle < 75°$	$60.00°$	-	$70.00°$	$61.78°$	14
3.	CARINATED SCRAPERS					
	Bit Width	1.40	-	2.30	1.75 cm	6
	Bit Convexity	.40	-	.80	.56 cm	6
	Bit $\angle$	$60.00°$	-	$88.00°$	$73.83°$	6

Table 3

LATE ARCHAIC SCRAPERS

	RANGE		MEAN	n
1. EXPANDED BIT SCRAPERS				
Length	2.00 -	4.60	3.03 cm	12
Width	1.50 -	2.70	2.03 cm	15
Thickness	.80 -	1.60	1.19 cm	15
Bit $\angle$	65.00° -	100.00°	79.80°	15
2. BIFACE SCRAPERS				
Length	1.90 -	3.40	2.64 cm	9
Width	1.50 -	2.60	1.93 cm	10
Thickness	.70 -	1.30	.96 cm	10
Bit $\angle$	55.00° -	85.00°	71.75°	8
3. ANGLED SCRAPERS				
Length	2.80 -	3.60	3.18 cm	5
Width	1.80 -	2.80	2.18 cm	6
Thickness	.70 -	1.80	1.11 cm	6
Bit $\angle$	55.00° -	63.00°	59.33°	6

Function

The three bits exhibit different degrees of wear, the most extreme being plate 71, with some step-flakes crushed off the bit. They are all end scrapers but may have been used on different materials.

Temporal and Spatial Distribution

The three were widely separated on the site, and all were in the lowest levels. This observation, together with the uniqueness of their forms, materials, and techniques, suggests that they may actually be older than the other artifacts in Stratum 5B. A fluted point was found in dune sands on the bluff above the Neville site. These small scrapers would be normal members of a Paleo-Indian assemblage. They may have been found on an older site and brought to Neville as attractive curiosities.

Miscellaneous Middle Archaic Scrapers

Sixteen thick flake scrapers from Strata 4B and 5 could not be described in any of the classes defined here. In most instances, technical or morphological attributes of the bits were outside the ranges included in the class definitions. The wide variability may be explicable on the basis of raw material alone, as 75% were of quartz, which is not amenable to standardization of forms.

In size, all fall within or very close to the limits of the steep flake scrapers. Ranges for the miscellaneous group are: lengths 1.4-4.2, maximum widths 1.5-3.4, maximum thicknesses .7-1.9.

The stratigraphic distribution is subsumed in the bar graph on figure 12. There was no significant clustering within the group.

Biface Scrapers

Technology

Ten small quartz bifaces were trimmed all around the peripheries. The bifaces taper from the bit, but at no consistent angle, and no haft element was defined.

Morphology

The bifaces have convex scraper bits near the point of maximum width. The four illustrated on plate 13a-d display the range of form. Dimensions are summarized on table 3. The mean L:W ratio is 1.3:1.

Function

These tools seem to have received heavy usage on hard materials. Three have been resharpened more than once, on alternate faces, and one is damaged on both faces. The tool may have been reversed in use, to minimize time-out for resharpening. Crushing of the bit, as illustrated on plate 23i, was observed on seven specimens. Crushed areas on the sides of the tool above the bit were observed on three specimens; such damage could have been caused by a bone socket haft, for which these tools are suitably shaped.

Temporal and Spatial Distribution

As shown on figure 12, these tools cluster in upper Stratum 4A. There was a group of four in square N5W1, including the specimen in Stratum 3. In N7, two nearly identical specimens were recovered, one from the overburden of Stratum 1. Therefore, 80-90% of them were *in situ* in Late Archaic levels at this site.

Deficiencies in the literature make comparisons difficult.

Expanded-bit Scrapers

Technology

These tools were made by steep unifacial flaking on thick spalls or flakes which were selected for trianguloid shape. The lateral edges were blunted by steep flaking or by flake scar remnants. The predominant material was quartz (86%); one specimen of rhyolite and one of chert complete the count.

Morphology

The tools so formed were thick unifacial scrapers with convex bits which are the widest part of the artifact. When the proximal end is present, it tapers. Three of the fifteen specimens are illustrated (pl. 13e-g); dimensions are summarized on table 3. The L:W ratio averages 1.5:1.

Function

The blunted sides make these implements suitable for use either in a socket haft or unhafted. There is no edge crushing to indicate that they were hafted. The bits have been used on hard materials; 60% are crushed from the ventral toward the dorsal surface. The wear is asymmetric on six of the nine damaged specimens — concentrating left of center on five, right on one — when the tool is oriented with the dorsal surface up, bit distal. Plate 23h illustrates characteristic bit damage. The wide range of bit angles on these tools, summarized on table 3, remains uninterpreted.

Temporal and Spatial Distribution

The stratigraphic position of thirteen out of the fifteen members of this class is shown on figure 12. They occurred at the 2/3 interface (6%), in Stratum 3 (60%), and near the 3/4A interface (20%). The deepest specimens, discontinuous from the main distribution, are very probably intrusive from above. Late Archaic associations are strongly indicated for these, as well as a temporal span beginning after the peak frequency of the bifacial scrapers.

   Extra-site distributions will not be considered because of deficiencies in the literature.

Angled Scrapers

Technology

Bifacial flaking dominates this type, for both body and bit shaping. In spite of this, the sections are plano-convex. The one uniface has a bifacially trimmed bit; one biface has a unifacially trimmed bit, perhaps representing an early stage of use before resharpening. Five of the six specimens were made of quartz, one of rhyolite.

Morphology

These are thick tools with a scraper edge shaped aslant the midline. The bits slant to the left when the specimens are oriented with the convex side up, bit distal. The dimensions are summarized on table 3. The L:W ratio is 1.4:1.

Function

The acute bit angles of this class are among the lowest on the site. Wear traces are minimal; these scrapers probably worked on soft materials. They may have been used for slicing and as side scrapers rather than end scrapers.

Temporal and Spatial Distribution

The small sample has a very diffuse distribution at the site. Two were in Stratum 2, one in Stratum 3, two at the 3/4 interface, and one in Stratum 4. They are probably of Late Archaic age, as their general resemblances to both biface scrapers and expanded-bit scrapers suggest.

Ovate Biface Scrapers

Technology

Six large ovate bifaces were flaked by percussion, apparently with soft hammers. On two felsite specimens, no further work was done. Four were made of an indurated tuff which now has chemically altered surfaces; these four have some bevel retouch on the edges. The flaking technique is fully comparable to Susquehanna tradition canons.

Morphology

One is illustrated on plate 9b. The lengths of four complete specimens range from 6.95 to 7.65 cm. The maximum widths were 2.65 to 3.30 cm, thicknesses .90 to 1.30 cm, for the six pieces.

Function

The broad, curved ends of all specimens show some wear and rounding from use, a wear pattern typical of large bifacial scrapers of the Susquehanna tradition. On two specimens the flake crests near the rounded end are also worn.

Temporal and Spatial Distribution

Three were at the 3/4A interface, one each in Strata 3 and 2 and one in a trench disturbance. Late Archaic period associations are indicated. All occurred at the south end of the excavated area, within and between the N3 and N-1 rows of squares.

The distribution of these artifacts within the Northeast is not well known, as unstemmed bifaces are underrepresented in the literature.

They are closely comparable to unstemmed biface scrapers occasionally seen in Atlantic and Watertown phase assemblages.

Miscellaneous Late Archaic Scrapers

Eight scrapers and scraper fragments from Strata 3 and 4A are unaccounted for above.

Two flake end scrapers of rhyolite were excavated from the middle levels of Stratum 4A, where they may have been associated with Brewerton points. Their dimensions are: lengths 3.9 and 3.4, widths 2.6 and 2.0, thicknesses .8 and 1.4, bit angles 65° and 60°, respectively.

Two irregular quartz specimens were probably aberrant expanded-bit and biface scrapers; their proveniences tend to confirm the tentative identifications.

The remaining four unifacial specimens, three of quartz and one of agate, are too small and incomplete for classification. All are under 2 cm long and only .4 to .6 cm thick. They were found in the lower half of Stratum 3.

Long-flake End Scrapers

Technology

All three scrapers of this class were made on long, ridged flakes which approached flake-blade dimensions. The bulbar end of two specimens had been snapped off; the scraper bits were pressure-flaked on the distal ends of the flakes. The materials were chert, felsite, and siltstone.

Morphology

Straight or barely convex scraper bits on the narrow ends of long flakes characterize this class. One of three is illustrated on plate 13m. Lengths range from 2.5 to 3.3 cm, maximum widths from 1.8 to 2.1 cm, thicknesses from .6 to .9 cm. Bit angles were 65°, 85°, and 85°.

Function

Two of the bits show end-scraper wear, one polished, one scarred (pl. 23i), The lateral edges of all three show damage from use. These may be compound cutting and scraping tools.

Temporal and Spatial Distribution

All three were recovered from Stratum 2, the eighteenth-century plow zone. Their absence below that zone is taken as evidence for Woodland period associations. They were found in the southern half of the main excavation area, in squares N2, N4, and N6. No comparisons have been made because of deficiencies in the literature.

Meadowood Scrapers

Two small triangular end scrapers on bifaces are identified as Meadowood scrapers by comparison with specimens in collections and the literature (e.g., Ritchie 1955, p. 35; 1969a, p. 183).

Technology

One specimen of black porphyry is so worn from use that the flaking cannot be analyzed. The second specimen was pressure-flaked of Deepkill chert from Hudson Valley formations. Both have scraper bits carefully shaped on the broad end. The point end of the porphyry specimen is a perforator.

Morphology

Both are illustrated on plate 13o and p. They have identical dimensions: lengths 2.3 cm, widths 1.8 cm, thicknesses .5 cm.

Function

The chert specimen has a few use-scars on the bit. The principle use of the porphyry specimen was as a perforator/reamer, as previously described.

Temporal and Spatial Distribution

Both were in Stratum 2, in the northern half of the main excavation area. Woodland associations are indicated by both the form and the stratigraphy.

Meadowood scrapers, like their associated artifacts, are distributed from the eastern Great Lakes to the Atlantic coast.

Miscellaneous Flake Scrapers

Four dissimilar flake scrapers from Stratum 2 remain to be described. The provenience suggests Woodland associations for them, but no close comparisons can be made.

One is a small triangle of green Deepkill chert, illustrated on plate 13n. All three edges have use damage.

A second scraper, of indurated tuff, has been shaped on an older, already patinated, flake. It is shown on plate 13l.

The bulbar end of a flake of indurated tuff has two scraper edges worked on it, one straight in configuration, one with a small nose. The specimen is almost square in outline and less than 2 cm in any dimension. Both edges were crushed in heavy use.

A thick quartzite spall with a steep convex scraper edge shows no wear marks. It could be a displaced, aberrant, Middle Archaic scraper.

CASUAL FLAKE TOOLS

Unstandardized trimmed flakes and flakes utilized without modification were combined for description when analysis indicated that similar morphological and functional attributes occur in both classes. On unstandardized tools, resharpening for continued use can rarely be distinguished from preliminary shaping of working edges. Therefore, there is no clear distinction between utilized raw flakes and flakes minimally modified for use.

Seventy-five percent of all such specimens were recovered below the 4A/4B interface, in the Middle Archaic zones. Those specimens were generally large flakes or spalls, often with thick cross sections. Primary flakes were favored, many having cortical surfaces. Core-rejuvenation flakes and wedge-shaped spalls and chunks are also strongly represented. The twenty-five percent from above the 4A/4B interface include biface-thinning flakes and flakes from prepared cores, which were rarely if ever utilized in the lower levels.

Scrapers

Twenty-seven casual flake tools (26%) have edge angles greater than 65° on the utilized margins. All but three such edges were intentionally trimmed. Scraper use is indicated by wear and breakage patterns like those observed on the standardized scrapers in the collection. There is no consistency of form or dimensions. One specimen is illustrated on plate 8h.

Seventy-four percent of these tools were in the Middle Archaic levels. They were shaped on heavy flakes selected for suitable edges and could not have been hafted. The edges frequently resemble those of the steep flake scrapers described above.

The specimens from above the 4A/4B interface are generally thinner, with finer edges, because of the different kinds of flakes selected.

Raw materials are predominantly various felsites (55%), followed by cherts (14%) which are all from upper levels, then Middle Archaic flakes of quartz (11%), quartzites (11%), and various argillaceous stones (7%).

Spokeshaves

Six flake tools with trimmed concave cutting edges were found in Middle Archaic levels. In addition to the five plotted on figure 13, one was in Stratum 5B of square N1E9. One is illustrated on plate 8f. All were made on thick flakes or chunks of rock, with the concavity steeply beveled to form a tough working edge. Various volcanics (66%) and quartzites (33%) were used.

Spokeshaves with steeply beveled edges formed on thick flakes are a minor element in eastern Paleo-Indian assemblages (e.g., Kraft 1973, p. 100; Dragoo 1973, p. 32). They are rarely described otherwise, so that comparisons with later assemblages are difficult.

Flake Knives

Seventy (67%) of the casual flake tools have been identified as knives because of morphological or functional attributes indicative of either slicing or shaving uses.

Technology

Retouch may precede or follow use, but it is rarely more than needed to regularize or sharpen the working edge, at angles less than 65°. Unifacial retouch predominates, more often dorsal than ventral. Bifacial edge retouch was observed on only six specimens. Raw materials were felsites (57%), argillites (15%), quartzites (12%), quartz (5%), and miscellaneous (8%).

Morphology

Most of these flakes (74%) are roughly wedge shaped in cross section, so that there is a plane-surfaced back opposite the cutting edge. Decortication flakes, core-rejuvenation flakes, spalls, and random chunks of rock were selected for these attributes. Only two specimens have intentional blunting retouch to back the knife edge. There is no other consistency of form. Specimens are illustrated on plate 8c, d, g, i. The other 26% are flake knives of miscellaneous forms, generally thinner than the wedge-shaped ones, and unbacked (pl. 8e).

Function

The predominant wedge form indicates that these implements were held so that pressure was applied on the back surface toward the cutting edge. The most commonly observed wear pattern was caused by friction along the cutting edge, which resulted in a crushed or worn edge. Chip damage, when present, was usually bifacial. Both slicing and shaving functions, involving both hard and soft materials, seem to be represented. The wear patterns were comparable on the wedge-shaped flakes and on the thin flakes. These tools may be equivalent to both knives and side-scrapers in other assemblages.

Temporal and Spatial Distribution

Seventy-six percent of these tools were below the 4A/4B interface (fig. 13), in Middle Archaic levels. These included all but five of the wedge-shaped specimens and only five of the simple flake knives.

The wedge-shaped knives are closely comparable to specimens from generally early contexts elsewhere in the East. Side-scrapers Types II and III at the Hardaway site are similar; they are associated with both Early and Middle Archaic assemblages there. The Middle Archaic Stanly and Morrow Mountain associations are especially relevant for comparison with the Neville assemblages (Coe 1964, p. 79). Similar tools appear in a Dalton context in Arkansas (Morse 1973, pp. 27-28).

The simple flake knives, which appear in small numbers throughout the Neville sequence, may be compared to similar unstandardized tools in assemblages of all ages, from Paleo-Indian to protohistoric times.

Choppers

Six unhafted tools made by minimal retouching of massive flakes and spalls were recovered from the Middle Archaic levels. One was at the Stratum 4A/B interface, three in 5A, and two in 5B. Two are illustrated on plate 17a, b. The forms are unstandardized except for the presence of transverse facets opposite the worn edges. These tools resemble other Middle Archaic flake tools — knives and scrapers — except for their much greater size. The two specimens from Stratum 5B have picklike working edges (pl. 17a). Those from 5A and 4A/B have convex working edges (pl. 17b), including one which is shaped like a thick scraper, with steep unifacial edge trimming. All were battered, with crushed areas and small flake scars along the working edges. The uppermost specimen differed in having most of its working edge rounded and smoothed. The scraperlike specimen resembles a pulping plane in form but was not used as a plane, having no wear on the flat surface. Igneous and metamorphic rocks were selected; one specimen was quartzite.

POLYHEDRAL NUCLEI

Fourteen small polyhedrons have been grouped into three classes, which seem to be culturally significant. The polyhedrons, being ungeometric, irregular three-dimensional forms, cannot meaningfully be represented in two-dimensional illustrations. All were made by repeated blows upon a block of stone, the material being rotated so that blows were struck from two or more plane surfaces. All were reduced to dimensions less than 3 cm in any diameter.

Two nuclei from Stratum 2 were formed by bipolar blows. The dimensions range from 2.2 cm maximum to .7 cm minimum. The materials were quartz crystal and jasper. These are the only specimens which resemble the *pièces esquillées* of Paleo-Indian assemblages.

Two nuclei from Stratum 5B were made of quartz crystal, flaked from several directions. The remaining cores range from 2.1 to 1.2 cm in diameter. All the crests between flake scars have been severely battered or crushed.

Nine polyhedrons from Stratum 4B and one from the 1/2 interface were made by blows from many directions against chunks of fine-grained volcanic rocks. The resulting pieces have diameters ranging from 2.9 to 1.2 cm; maxima average 2.7 cm, minima average 1.7 cm. Six of these specimens show no use-wear. Four have small scraperlike noses chipped from one plane surface, with bit angles between 80° and 85°. The noses resemble the beaks of beaked scrapers except that they are smaller in all dimensions and have steeper bit angles. Three of the four nosed specimens were recovered between 48 and 51 inches deep, the fourth just below 51 inches. There is no horizontal cluster of these artifacts on the site, nor any consistent association with other artifacts. No comparable objects are known to me.

FLAKING DEBRIS

Middle Archaic Biface Preforms

A large number of biface fragments excavated from the Middle Archaic levels of the site appear as a special class of chipping waste. Efforts to count and classify the fragments were abandoned because of classification problems and constraints on available time. General remarks only will be offered here. Fragments of this sort were almost as numerous as projectile points below the 4A/4B interface and fairly evenly distributed.

Technology

All the flake scars were made by percussion flaking with cylinder hammers. Only one quartzite specimen had any retouch on the edges (pl. 6f). Progressive thinning and shape refinement are indicated by the fact that the smaller specimens are the more regular in shape and surface. Raw materials were predominantly rhyolite; other volcanics, argillites, and quartzites were also used.

Morphology

One end of these bifaces was pointed, the other was convex or nearly straight (pl. 6c, e, f). Cross sections were usually thick and irregular. The lengths of specimens which could be measured in that dimension ranged downward from 10 cm to around 6 cm. Maximal widths ranged from 5.2 to 2.4 cm, and maximal thickness ranged from 1.6 to 6 cm. Because of flaws in the stone or misplaced hammer blows, almost all had broken during flaking. Nearly intact specimens had been discarded for flaws which prevented further thinning. The one piece which appears to have been completed before breakage was a uniquely fine specimen of quartzite (pl. 6f).

Function

The absence of retouch and use-wear on these fragments is indicative of their status as manufacturing waste, material spoiled at an early stage of production. Along with the quantities of flake debris on the site, they represent a major stone-knapping industry at this location. They were probably projectile point preforms, since no other major class of bifacially flaked tools was represented here.

Temporal and Spatial Distribution

The two shapes of the bases, convex and almost straight, compare well with the two kinds of Middle Archaic quarry blades at the Doerschuk site. Coe's Types I and II quarry blades have Stanly and Morrow Mountain associations in the Uwharrie sequence (Coe 1964, pp. 50-51), equivalent to the Neville and Stark associations here.

Workshops

Two concentrations of flaking waste were recognized during excavation and separated from the general excavation-unit collections. They represent incomplete samples of debris from two workshops. It is not known whether the materials were in pits.

A workshop from square N8 at 63 to 66 inches in Stratum 5B consisted of debris representing two grades of rhyolite. A talus slab, fractured by natural forces, is of coarse-grained material and is unworked. There is a small chunk of fine-grained rhyolite abandoned after some preliminary striking platform preparation. A tip fragment of a large thick biface, a medial fragment of a small biface, and thirty-eight flakes with platforms complete the inventory. The striking platforms are all biface edges, lipped, with little or no hammer damage. The bulbs of percussion are diffuse. Cylinder hammer percussion is indicated, employed in progressive biface thinning. The largest ten flakes include some with cortex surfaces and thick sections. The remaining twenty-eight range in size from 3.0 x 2.5 cm to small flakes less than 1.5 cm in any dimension. The smallest flakes closely correspond to the size and shape of surface scars on Neville points. This association of debris appears to be waste from the production of something like Neville points.

The second workshop, from square N2E1 at 57 to 60 inches, consists of twenty-one flakes with platform ends, flake fragments, and one tetrahedral chunk of talus debris. The material is rhyolite of two distinct grades of graininess. The flakes were derived from at least two cores, distinguished by both texture and cortex color. The tetrahedron has some flake scars resulting from attempts to convert it into a biface. The attempts failing, the piece was discarded. Sixteen of the flakes were biface-shaping debris with thick sections. The remaining five were biface-thinning flakes. All extant striking platforms were on biface edges or equally acute angles with one cortical surface. All platforms are lipped and show no crushing or roughening. Bulbs are diffuse. As in the N8 workshop, biface shaping and thinning with cylinder hammers is indicated. In this instance, the product was a biface preform rather than a projectile point.

Waste Flakes

Because of limitations of time and trained manpower, waste-flake analysis was not pursued very far. Flake counts and raw material distributions were reasonably consistent in all the undisturbed squares, so that the case of square N3W1, shown in figure 7, is typical.

In spite of the high flake counts in most levels, especially in Strata 4B and 5, the samples of measurable flakes were small. The percentages of extant striking platforms on flakes in the Middle Archaic levels averaged around 11%, being generally higher for volcanic stones and much lower for quartz.

Measurements of platform angles in three squares, N1E2, N3W1, and N8, confirmed the visual impression that most of the debris represented biface-thinning flakes, with modal flake: platform angles between 103° and 108°. A significant secondary mode showed up among the quartz flakes, around 92°. While this angle may be controlled by quartz fracture properties, it may also represent intentional smashing of quartz to produce the thick chunky fragments favored for some scrapers. The selection of thick flakes and chunks of all material for flake tools tended to bias the remaining debris toward overrepresentation of thin flakes.

No study of debris above the 4A/4B interface was attempted, because of complications in the natural and cultural stratification.

GROUND STONE TOOLS

Axes

One full-grooved axe and a preform for a second were recovered in Middle Archaic contexts.

Technology

The three techniques employed to shape and finish the axes — flaking, pecking, and grinding — are shown in the illustration. Nothing about the manufacturing techniques distinguishes these from full-grooved axes from Late Archaic assemblages. The materials are medium-grained mafic igneous rocks.

Morphology

They are illustrated on plate 15. The major dimensions are as follows, with the completed axe listed first: lengths 16.4 and 18.7 cm, widths 10.8 and 9.6 cm, thicknesses 5.9 and 4.6 cm. There is no lipping at the groove margins of either piece.

Function

Both faces of the completed specimen show use damage. Small chips scar the bit, and striae run upward from the bit at an angle of about 20° from the axis of the tool. Diagonal striations are characteristic of a tool hafted and swung as an axe (Semenov 1964, p. 129).

Temporal and Spatial Distribution

The two specimens were recovered at deep levels in the site; this suggests Middle Archaic associations. Because of the great interest of such an early context for full-grooved axes, the stratigraphic relationships in the two squares involved were checked by every available means.

In square N4, the completed axe was first noticed between 54 and 57 inches, where it was recorded as a "large stone in SE corner." It was not identified until the 60- to 63-inch level was excavated. The axe lay on the 5A/B interface, near and above Neville points. The levels which enclosed it contained Stark and Merrimack points. A charcoal sample from the 54-inch level gave a radiocarbon age of 7,210±140 years, which should be a minimal age for the axe.

The preform from square N3W1 was bagged with material from the 51- to 54-inch level, but not otherwise recorded. The north wall profile in figure 4 shows that this level corresponds to the 4B/5A interface for part of the area but is interrupted by a large pit on the west side. The axe's exact location being unknown, it cannot be assigned confidently to either Stratum 4B or 5A. Stark and Merrimack points were recovered above and in the square east of the axe unit; both Merrimack and Neville points were bagged with it. There is no evidence for any deep disturbance which could have intruded the axe from above Stratum 4B. It is at least older than the 4A/B interface, which is dated by two C14 samples close to 6,000 years old.

These full-grooved axes are the oldest so far reported in the East. Their seventh and eighth millennial ages are comparable to ages attributed to early full-grooved axes in the Midwest, at Graham Cave and Modoc Rockshelter (summarized in Coe 1964, p. 122). Some eastern full-grooved axes thus have an antiquity far greater than has been assumed for them; they can no longer be considered a horizon style of the Late Archaic period.

Gouges and Adzes

Gouges

Five gouges were represented by four bit fragments and one medial fragment. Four were of basalt, one of flow-banded felsite. Two bit fragments are illustrated on plate 14g and h. Plate 14g bears evidence for a sequence of manufacturing techniques from flaking, to pecking, to grinding. Bits were sharpened by whetting transversally on the dorsal surface and axially on the ventral surface. Three of the bits have chip scars; one is worn smooth on both surfaces, without striations.

Two of the bit fragments were recorded at depths indicative of Stratum 5 provenience. In both cases, however, the squares involved are known to have been deeply disturbed, and the bag notes are insufficiently detailed for confidence in such early provenience. The other two bits were in Late Archaic levels in Stratum 4A and at the 3/4 interface. The medial fragment was in Stratum 2.

Adze

A single adze bit fragment was recorded from levels corresponding to Stratum 4B in square N1. The profile of that square shows a large pit intruding to that depth from Stratum 3. A small broken quartz point was recovered with the adze, increasing the probability of intrusion there.

Fragments

Three fragments of ground stone tools, either gouges or adzes, complete the inventory. Two were from Stratum 4A. A poll fragment with one flattened surface was reported from Stratum 5, in the square adjacent to the deepest gouge bit. The possibility of intrusion is less in this instance, where the excavator recorded the base of the intrusive trench well above the level of the poll. However, doubts remain, and there is no firm case for Middle Archaic gouges or adzes at this site.

Atlatl Weights

Two morphological classes of atlatl weights — winged and ovoid — are represented in the collection. No complete specimen of either class was recovered.

Middle Archaic Winged Weights

Eight fragments represent seven different winged atlatl weights. Six of these were on or below the 4A/B interface in the Middle Archaic zones. Four were in or on Stratum 4B, including the specimen illustrated on plate 14c, which was recovered from two separate squares. Individual wing fragments occurred also in Stratum 5B and at the 5A/B interface.

Manufacturing techniques are poorly represented on fragments of finished implements. One specimen shows pecking scars incompletely obliterated by the grinding and polishing which was the final manufacturing step. Two fragments have rotary drill striations in the central perforation; on one of those and on one other, longitudinal striations mark the final stage of perforation. One small unique specimen seems to have been a practice piece or a toy, broken during manufacture. Its surface was finished before it was drilled, and drilling was begun from both ends of the centrum. The rounded ends of the drilled holes indicate that the drill shaft was solid, probably of organic material, and used with an added abrasive.

The wing fragments have either lenticular (4) or parallelogram (1) cross sections. Three have one curved and one straight edge; two have two curved edges. Edges were either faceted (4) or ridged (2); faceting when present was restricted to the straight edge except on one specimen. There is no other significant pairing of these alternative attributes.

Four specimens were made of fine-grained banded or foliaceous metamorphic rocks, and two were of felsitic porphyries.

The forms, to the extent that they can be observed, resemble the semilunar form of Coe's Stanly type atlatl weights from the Hardaway and Doerschuk sites (Coe 1964, pp. 53, 81). At the Neville site, the associations of the winged weights are primarily the Merrimack and Stark points which dominate Stratum 4B. Associations with Neville points in Stratum 5 cannot be confirmed on the basis of only two wing fragments.

Late Archaic Winged Weight

The seventh winged weight, represented by a wing-tip fragment of tuffaceous banded slate, was recovered in the lower part of Stratum 3 in square N1E2. The form of the fragment specifically resembles the faceted-edge winged atlatl weights which are typical of the Atlantic phase in southeastern New England (Dincauze 1972, Plate VIII 1). The stratigraphic and spatial associations of this fragment lend weight to such an identification (see chapter 3).

Ovoid Weight

Only one ovoid weight of indurated tuff has been identified (pl. 14b). It was made by grinding after initial pecking. The perforation was rotary drilled then finished by longitudinal grinding. The provenience at the Strata 2/3 interface is indicative of Late Archaic associations.

Miscellaneous Fragments

Two additional perforated atlatl weights of banded slates are represented only by centrum fragments. One was in Stratum 4B, the other in 4A.

Ground Slates

Ulus

Fragments of two comb-back ulus were recovered. The largest piece (pl. 14f) came from the fill of the deep trench in N14W1, so that it lacks useful provenience. It was used and resharpened after breaking. A fragment from the upper corner of a second ulu was found in the upper part of Stratum 4A in the middle of the Late Archaic levels. No cultural associations are indicated for these pieces.

Slate Pendant

A perforated, semicircular pendant was recovered in several pieces from two adjacent squares (pl. 14d). Most of the fragments were in Stratum 2; the deepest, at 27 inches, was probably in a pit intruding Stratum 3. Woodland associations are the most probable.

Slab Knives

Two thin slabs of phyllite have been modified by bifacial grinding along convex cutting edges (pl. 14a). Maximal thicknesses are between .25 and .3 cm. Both are broken in other dimensions. Neither edge is very sharp; the illustrated specimen has short striations impinging onto one face and perpendicular to the edge. These were recovered from the lower part of Stratum 4A in two widely separated squares. In one case, two Otter Creek points were in an adjacent square at the same level; in the other, a Brewerton Eared-Notched point was in the same excavation unit.

Miscellaneous Fragments

Spalled and broken fragments of five other slate artifacts could not be interpreted. They are mentioned only because of their stratigraphic clustering.

Two flat fragments with ground edges, which might be fragments of atlatl weights, are from the upper part of Stratum 4B. Three spalls with at least one smooth surface are from lower Stratum 3. Two of them have portions of round holes at a broken edge.

HAMMERS

Pebble Hammers

Seven pebble hammers with battered ends were all recovered from Stratum 5.

Technology

River pebbles of suitable size and material were probably obtained locally at the foot of the falls. Dense igneous rocks such as diorite were favored; the single exception was of quartzite (pl. 16b). The selection criteria were apparently rigid; in the same stratum with the hammers were eleven unused granite pebbles all of which proved to be all slightly smaller than the hammers.

Morphology

Table 4 presents the basic dimensions. Two are illustrated on plate 16b and c; the orientation is polar through the battered areas.

Function

The pebbles have both cut and peck scars on the ends, such as would be formed in use against hard, angular material. It was impossible to show a specific function, but it may be significant that these hammers occur in the levels which include the early peak of quartz flaking debris. All but one have scars on both ends. The wide variation in weights indicates that specific gravity was not among the criteria of selection.

Temporal and Spatial Distribution

These hammers occur only in Stratum 5, where they are associated with Neville points. They have been reported at only one other site, Pine Ridge Cemetery in Tewksbury, Massachusetts. There, they were found, along with a small point that may be a Neville, in the lowest cultural level (Vossberg 1959, p. 38, nos. 30, 31).

Core Hammers

Morphology

Ten quartz chunks with severe battering damage appear to have been used as hammerstones. The battering is concentrated on crests between flake scars or on natural angles of the piece. Some may be exhausted flake cores, but in all cases the battering damage far exceeds that characteristic of simple nuclei. One is illustrated on plate 16a. There are two distinct size ranges with stratigraphic separation. Four specimens from Stratum 5 ranged in lengths from 6.0 to 6.5 cm, in widths from 4.5 to 6.4 cm, in thicknesses from 3.0 to 5.6 cm, and in weight from 116.5 to 303.6 gm. Three specimens from Stratum 4B were smaller: lengths 3.3 to 3.8 cm, widths 2.6 to 3.3 cm, thicknesses 1.0 to 2.6 cm, weight 38.3 to 75.1 gm. The remaining three specimens from Strata 4A and 1 (two examples) are somewhat more variable, falling outside these ranges one or more dimensions.

Function

The hardness of the stone, the battered edges, and the hard use are what would be expected of pecking tools used to shape heavy stone tool blanks.

Angular Cobble Hammers

Technology

The cobbles selected for hammerstone use were subangular river cobbles of igneous (11) or metamorphic (1) rocks, quartz and quartzite (4).

Morphology

This class includes all those cobbles with hammer damage concentrated on angular projections. They are all casual tools, showing only modification by use. Table 4 summarizes the major dimensions of twelve out of sixteen such specimens. Two were too broken to measure, and the two largest examples were excluded from the summary because of their extremity and special provenience. They were both recovered near the 4A/B interface; one was in Feature 14, as shown in plate 2a. The dimensions of the extreme examples were: lengths 11.8 and 14.5 cm, widths 8.5 and 12.7 cm, thicknesses 6.8 and 8.6 cm, weight 1036 and 2464 gm, respectively, with the Feature 14 specimen listed second.

Function

These were heavy-duty hammerstones. Battering, crushing, linear scars, and spalling damage were observed; they were often combined on single specimens. They may have been used for the initial quartering of raw materials for chipped stone tools.

TABLE 4

DIMENSIONS OF HAMMERS

		RANGE	MEAN	s	n
1.	PEBBLE HAMMERS				
	Length	5.00 - 6.80	5.85 cm	.66	7
	Width	3.82 - 5.30	4.21 cm	.51	7
	Thickness	2.55 - 4.90	3.55 cm	.75	6
	Weight	72.0 - 229.5 gm	—	—	6
2)	ANGULAR COBBLE HAMMERS				
	Length	5.80 - 11.00	8.29 cm	2.00	12
	Width	4.30 - 9.60	6.17 cm	.53	12
	Thickness	3.00 - 6.00	4.23 cm	.54	12
	Weight	185.90 - 728.00	350.50 cm	202.30	12

Temporal and Spatial Distribution

These tools were recovered from all strata except 1 and 5A. There was only one in Stratum 2, two in Stratum 3, five in Stratum 4A, two in 4B, and five in 5B. They were observed in Features 14, 23, and 35. Both Late Archaic and Middle Archaic associations are indicated.

Discoid Cobble Hammers

Five discoid cobble hammers with battering continuous around the periphery were distinguished from the angular cobble hammers; these may be only special instances of a more inclusive cobble hammer class. The materials chosen were similar, the dimensions fall within the ranges of the angular cobble hammers, and, again, the largest and heaviest specimen was at the 4A/B interface. Three specimens were in Stratum 4A, and only one in 5B, at the base. Thus, they are more characteristic of the Late Archaic assemblages than of earlier ones.

PEBBLE TOOLS

Notched and Grooved Pebbles

Two full-grooved pebbles were collected at the Stratum 4A/B interface in squares N5 and N1E3. Both are ovoid river pebbles of granite and are grooved around the longest circumference by pecking (pl. 16e). The dimensions are: lengths 5.5 and 4.9 cm, widths 4.5 and 3.8 cm, thicknesses 3.7 and 3.0 cm. The grooves are shallow and broad, not the best shape for seating a cord; but sinew wrapping might hold firmly.

A third pebble of gneiss is of similar size and shape. It was found in the lower part of Stratum 4A in N1E2, four to six inches above the floor on which the grooved pebbles lay. It is notched at the ends (pl. 16d).

ABRADERS

Middle Archaic Levels

Tabular Abraders

Seven slabs of gritty rocks from Strata 4B and 5 are included here. One is illustrated (pl. 17c). All are tuffs, more or less metamorphosed. At least one surface of each has been worn smooth by abrasion; the edges of four are very smooth, perhaps from handling. Only on one is the worn face striated; the rest seem to have been used against soft material, which did not scratch the stone. An additional two specimens from disturbed contexts compare closely to the others, and probably were derived from the lower levels of the site.

Three additional slabs of tuffaceous slaty rock from Stratum 5B resemble the abraders but show no sign of utilization.

Friable Cylinders

Four pieces of gritty rocks — three of crystalline metamorphics and one of tuff — are subcylindrical in shape. At least two were pecked to achieve the shape. Maximal diameters range from 5.0 to 6.5 cm; minimal, from 3.9 to 4.8 cm. The only unbroken piece is 11.6 cm long; the others are shorter. Observations of use-wear are not possible on the friable surfaces. The similarity in size, shape, and material characteristics suggests that these were intended for some special use. One was at the 4A/B interface, one in Stratum 5A, and two were within 6 vertical inches of each other in Stratum 5B, in square N8E1.

Miscellaneous

A small piece of slate from Stratum 5B is illustrated on plate 14e. As it does not appear to be part of a larger artifact, it may have been a hone for tools of bone or antler. A second rounded piece of smoothed slate was recovered from the same level in an adjacent square. A small piece of tuff with three smoothed surfaces was nearby to the east.

Late Archaic Levels

A flaked rectangular piece of tuff from Stratum 3 has smoothed edges with longitudinal striae. It is broken off at one end. Its identification and use are unknown.

A small slab of fine-grained schistose rock from Stratum 4A has limonite adhesions on both faces. It comes from the same level and square (N1E3-39) as a lump of ocherous clay and may have been used to grind pigment.

Stratum 2

A carefully shaped whetstone of phyllite, rectangular in shape, has longitudinal striations on all surfaces. It is 3.2 cm wide, 1.1 cm thick, and broken off at 7.5 cm long. Both faces are slightly convex; the sides are parallel. It may be a Colonial tool, dropped in the plow zone.

PIGMENTS

Ocher

Four pieces of earthy yellow ocher were recovered from Stratum 4A. Three occurred in the southernmost row of squares.

Graphite

Fourteen lumps of graphite were catalogued, ranging between 15 and 66 inches below the surface. Seven of the pieces came from three adjacent squares (N1E1, N1E2, and N-1E2), each piece at a different level. A large rodent burrow existed in that part of the site and could account for the vertical range of all these pieces. Otherwise, there is graphite from the middle of Stratum 4A in two separate squares and from upper Stratum 3 in two separate layers. Late Archaic assocations are probable.

NONARTIFACTUAL MATERIALS

Forty-five pieces of rock with no evidence of utilization were collected. There is, therefore, an undefined sampling bias involved, which precludes the drawing of firm conclusions about distributions.

Roughly half of the sample (twenty-one specimens) are whole or fragmentary river cobbles. (Cobbles are here defined as naturally rounded rocks larger than 7 cm in at least one dimension.) Such pieces were either absent or not collected from Strata 1, 2, and 3. There are four from 4A, three each from 4B and 5A, and eight from 5B, including one in Feature 23. Various igneous and metamorphic rocks are represented. Only one is definitely burned, but many are broken by thermal spalling.

Sixteen pebbles (rounded stones less than 7 cm in any dimension) were collected. One is from Stratum 1, two from Stratum 3, one from 4B, and six each from 5A and 5B. Ten of the twelve from Stratum 5 resemble the pebble hammers from the same stratum, but they are slightly smaller and all but one is of granite, a rock not used for the hammers. The other pebbles are variable in size, shape, and material.

The remaining eight pieces are fragments of various foliaceous rocks with no stratigraphic clustering.

ABORIGINAL CERAMICS

Stratigraphic and Spatial Relationships

Over 1,200 sherds of unglazed aboriginal ceramics were recovered. The total count is not especially significant, since many of the pieces were small — under 2 cm in any dimension. Decorated sherds and all rimsherds were studied individually, in order to quantify some of the attributes and to approximate the range of variability within the sample. Plain and cord-marked bodysherds which had no other decoration were not analyzed. Rimsherds and decorated bodysherds were sorted into sets which were sufficiently consistent to represent single vessels. Most of the vessel lots contained only one sherd, but several were considerably more populous. Fifty-six discrete vessels were recognized among the rimsherds and fifty-one among the bodysherds. Two of the bodysherd vessel lots could be confidently assigned to two of the rimsherd vessels. A vessel count between sixty and seventy is probably a reasonable approximation of the total represented in the excavated area.

Figure 11 shows the stratigraphic distribution of all the sherds, including those known to have come from disturbed contexts. The buried plow zone, Stratum 2, contained between 32% and 42% of all the sherds excavated (boundary indeterminacies account for the uncertainty). None of the sherds below Stratum 2 is in its correct stratigraphic position; all were intruded into Archaic occupation levels by aboriginal pits or by later pits and trenches. This conclusion was established carefully by detailed comparison of excavation records, including notes, drawings, and photographs, and by checking the associations of deep sherds. In some instances, sherds from single vessels could be traced downward from Stratum 2 through several levels within a square. Furthermore, there is no stratigraphic correlation of any attribute or set of attributes outside of Stratum 2. Feature 41, in which rocker-stamped sherds and a corner-notched point were associated, was identified in the course of this stratigraphic analysis (pl. 20). In all other cases, it was impossible to be certain whether one or several intrusive pits were present in squares where sherds were recovered below Stratum 2.

The horizontal distribution of sherds in the excavated area is not random; the great majority of the sherds were found in and west of the main north-south trench. Squares to the east had far fewer sherds and fewer sherd-filled pits in them. The arrangement appears to be a product of prehistoric activity patterning; it was not caused by the eighteenth- and nineteenth-century intrusions.

The Neville site was not an important Amoskeag site during the Woodland period. Sometime during the Late Archaic period, the main focus of settlement and activity had shifted away from the Neville site, on the first terrace, to the Smyth site on the bluff, immediately above and east. The excavations of the New Hampshire Archeological Society and Franklin Pierce College at the Smyth site must be the main source of data on prehistoric life at Amoskeag during the Late Archaic and Woodland periods.

Attributes

No detailed report of the attribute analysis will be given, because few conclusions of any consequence could be drawn from it. The lack of stratigraphic data, the small size of the sherds, and the low number of sherds per vessel restrict the utility of the Neville sherd sample. Some

informative and potentially useful observations will be summarized below, as any description of New Hampshire ceramics may be helpful in
the current state of ignorance. The Smyth site collection would provide
a firm beginning for understanding the ceramics of southern New Hampshire.

The Neville ceramics had typical New England temper classes — grit,
sand, and shell. Medium to fine grit temper (< 2mm) predominated,
characterizing 62.5% of the rimsherd vessels and 49.0% of the bodysherd vessels. The second most frequent class was sand temper, 23.2%
of rims and 27.4% of bodysherd vessels. Shell temper followed, with
frequencies of 8.7% and 11.7%, respectively. Coarse grit temper and
mica temper were present in low frequencies, the latter appearing only
once in each set of vessels.

Vessel forms could be reconstructed in only one instance. The rocker-
stamped, grit-tempered pot illustrated on plate 21 had a slightly con-
stricted neck below an everted lip and an elongated body. Among all
the rimsherds, the form could be determined for less than half (46.4%).
Among these there was roughly equal representation of straight lips
(19.6%), everted lips (12.5%), and narrow collars (14.5%), all of the latter being less than 1.5 cm high. Flat lips far outnumbered other forms
(71.4%); rounded lips at 19.6%, and pointed lips at 5.3% complete the
count.

A wide variety of impressed and incised decorative techniques were
employed. Plain and cord-marked bodysherds were not counted. Parallel cord impressions (19.6%) and incision (26.8%) were the most common techniques on rimsherds. Motifs varied; some are illustrated on
plate 19. A dominant trait for lip decoration was a series of incised or
impressed nicks around the interior and/or exterior edge of flat lips
(32.1%). Rocker-stamping occured on 5.3% of rimsherds, on 21.5% of
decorated neck and bodysherd vessel lots. Dentate rocker and plain
dentate stamping were observed only on neck and bodysherds.

The vessel lots, once defined, were carefully compared to pottery
types already in the literature. Only two established types were represented — Vinette I (pl. 19a) and probably Chance Incised (pl. 19k)
(Ritchie and MacNeish 1949, p. 100; Lenig 1965, p. 6). Otherwise, the
vessels differed from established types in one or more crucial attributes.
On the whole, the vessels are all clearly within greater Northeastern pottery traditions, sharing attributes with vessels found to the west in New
York state, to the east in coastal Maine, and to the south in Massachusetts. Early Woodland vessels are represented by Vinette I and related
pots which lack the corded interiors. Middle Woodland rocker- and den-
tate-stamped vessels are present, including some with careless incision
combined with stamping (pl. 19d, l, n, o; pl. 20).

A large number of discrete vessels display attribute combinations typical of the early Late Woodland period in neighboring regions. Cord-impressed motifs, cord-wrapped stick impressions, and corded and simple punctations on narrow collars are attributes shared with Owasco and Oak Hill ceramics to the west as well as with southern New England ceramics (Dincauze 1975) (pl. 19b, c, e, g). The Neville vessels do not correspond closely to types defined elsewhere and are considered to be native products. Still later styles of decoration may be seen in fine incised designs on collared vessels and in fine cord-marking on thin body-sherds. Again, most of the thin-walled, narrow-collared vessels were probably local products, but some few sherds with Chance-related motifs may have been brought from farther west (pl. 19f, h, i, j, k, m).

FEATURES

Excavation and Analysis

Excavation procedures, as summarized in chapter 1, were not conducive to the recognition and recording of features. Such pits, hearths, and postholes as were recognized were noted on the level bags. They were sometimes sketched, rarely measured, and never assigned field numbers. Artifacts from features were usually bagged with the rest of the level, sometimes described well enough to be separated later. Occasional soil samples were saved; charcoal was collected but not always kept discrete by feature. Feature recognition varied among the excavators, squares, and strata. Between one and six features were recorded in sixteen of thirty-four squares — 47% of the major excavation units. Recognition required strong color contrast, which was present in the lighter colored sediments of Stratum 5 and in the lenses at the Stratum 4A/B interface, but was rare elsewhere. Most of the recognized features, therefore, were in the Middle Archaic levels of the site.

During analysis of the excavated materials, feature records were assembled from bag notes and photographs. A total of forty-seven feature numbers were assigned as features were identified, and a catalogue was compiled. Later it became evident that in two cases duplicate numbers had been assigned to single features at different levels within a square. The corrected total, therefore, is forty-five features, including one (No. 27) which is a large rodent burrow.

Ten classes of features were defined, not all of which are equally distinctive. These are: pits containing charcoal but no stones, hearths or pits with charcoal and hammerstones, charcoal concentrations with no record of pits, charcoal concentrations with granite and schist fragments, a group of cobbles with charcoal, a concentration of charred nuts, a deposit of calcined bone, pits containing pink ash, postmolds, and the rodent burrow. Soil samples from features were screened in the laboratory in hopes of recovering plant remains, but none were present.

Descriptions

Pits with Charcoal, no Stones

The twenty-one members of this class were recovered at or below the 4A/B interface. Eighteen of them were in Stratum 5B, the majority being recognized as they intruded the alluvial deposits below the cultural levels. Diameters, estimated from rough sketches without scale, ranged from one to two feet. Depths were measured only into the alluvium except for the three pits shown on the N3W1 profile in figure 4. Six- to eight-inch depths were probably typical. No records report whether or not the bases and sides of these pits were burned, but they were usually called fire pits. Soil samples were composed of charcoal, ash, and sand. Chipping debris was present in at least seven features. Charcoal from Feature 11 had a radiocarbon age of 7,650±400 years.

Hearths or Pits with Hammerstones

Two features in Stratum 5B had angular cobble hammerstones associated with charcoal; both were intrusive into the alluvium in the southern area of the excavation (N3E1 and N1E2). The larger of the two, Feature 23 in N1E2, contained two broken cobbles in addition to the hammer. Charcoal from this feature was 7,015±160 radiocarbon years old.

Charcoal without Recorded Pit

Three of the five features in this class were at the Stratum 4A/B interface; one each was in Strata 3 and 5B. This class may have nothing more in common than inadequate records. Charcoal collected from Feature 10 in square N4, at the 4A/B interface, was 5,910±180 years old.

Charcoal with Granite and Schist

The three features in this class occurred near the 3/4 interface, in Stratum 5A, and intrusive into alluvium from 5B. Feature 2 at the 3/4 interface resembled features of the previous class except that the charcoal spread included eight pieces of broken granite and schist, with diameters ranging from 3 to 8 inches. In Stratum 5A, a similar association of nine stones was recorded, again without any obvious pattern. This feature extended through two 3-inch levels and was assigned two feature numbers before the integrity of the rock association was recognized. From the upper of the two levels, charcoal was collected which was 7,740±280 radiocarbon years old. The deepest feature of this class contained two 5-inch long pieces of mica schist, placed on edge in charcoal-stained pit fill at the base of square N5W1.

Cobble Arrangement

Feature 14, which lay on the Stratum 4A/B interface in squares N5 and N6, is illustrated on plate 2a. The only cobble saved was an angular cobble hammerstone, the largest from the site. The others were discarded because of their size and lack of obvious use-wear. Charcoal was associated; the excavators called this feature a fireplace but did not report whether or not any of the stones were burned.

Charred Nuts

A small hearth feature was collected from the exposed south face of N2E2 at 36 inches below the surface. It consisted of a mass of burned nut shells and a couple of small burned stones. The collector reported the feature as a hearth *in situ* at 36 inches and expected that the sample would provide a good radiocarbon age for the Brewerton Eared-Notched points in the square adjacent to the south. A color photograph of the wall where the sample was removed shows no evidence of intrusion. The radiocarbon age of 3025±185 is too young to be associated with the Brewerton points. Furthermore, it is younger than two other charcoal samples from nearby squares at comparable depths. The charred nuts are hickory.

Calcined Bone

A deposit of small fragments of burned bone was recognized at the base of Stratum 4B in N5. The pieces are too small for identification.

Pits with Pink Ash

Three pits intrusive into Strata 3 and 4A from Stratum 2 were recognized because of a lens of pink ash near their bottoms. The pit walls were not traced, but the association of all three with pottery, and a young radiocarbon age for one, confirms their Stratum 2 provenience. The largest and deepest extended to 36 inches in square N3W1, about a foot below Stratum 2. This pit, Feature 41, was over a foot in diameter and contained 4 to 6 inches of pink ashy material at its base. Sherds from at least two different grit-tempered, rocker-stamped vessels were included in the fill. The association of a corner-notched point with this pit is highly probable but not conclusively demonstrated in the records. Two large sherds from one vessel and the projectile point are illustrated on plates 19n and 20a, b. A second pit with pink ash, associated with small grit-tempered, cord-marked sherds, was recognized in a corner of square N2E1. It extended into three adjoining squares where it was not recorded. A third pink ash feature (No. 19) was recorded at the west edge of square N6, just below Stratum 2 and adjacent to the large intrusive trench (fig. 3). The ash lay on charcoal which had a radiocarbon age of 395±90 years. No samples of the pink ash deposits were saved. The evidence demonstrates the Woodland affiliation of these features but is inadequate to explain their origin or function.

Postmolds

A Colonial period postmold, 8 inches in diameter, was recorded in square N3E2, 6 inches south of a shallow trench at that location. The trench and posthold intruded Stratum 3 to total depths of 27 inches and were truncated above by the plow zone which created Stratum 2. Neither could have been much more than a foot deep when dug from the seventeenth-century ground surface. No comparable features were recognized in other squares.

At the base of square N3, stained areas recorded as "3 fireplaces" were redefined at greater depth as "5 postmolds"; they were 3 to 5 inches in diameter, 12 to 13 inches apart. The postmolds were recognized as intrusive stains in the alluvium. The notes report that four of the stains formed an "arc," but no sketch or detailed measurements were made.

Feature 22 is an unequivocal postmold at the base of the cultural deposits. A sharpened stick was thrust into the alluvium below Stratum 5B, deforming some stained layers which are not otherwise recorded (pl. 2b). The mold was first recognized at the base of 5B, 69 inches deep. The photo shows the mold pedestaled and sectioned, extending below the 75-inch excavation floor. The postmold was removed intact and wrapped in plastic; it remains so in storage.

Burrow

At the southern end of the excavation, one or more very deep and large rodent burrows were recorded in squares N1, N1E1, N2E1, and N-1E2. They extend to the base of the cultural sequence from an unknown original surface. The largest continuous segment of burrow was given a feature number for ease of reference. Its presence is believed to explain the unusual vertical distribution of graphite fragments in these particular squares.

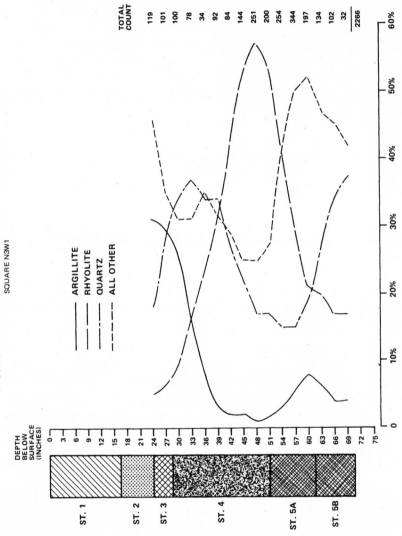

FIGURE 7   RAW MATERIAL FREQUENCY IN CHIPS
SQUARE N3W1

ARGILLITE
RHYOLITE
QUARTZ
ALL OTHER

TOTAL
COUNT

119
101
100
78
34
92
84
144
251
200
254
344
197
134
102
32

2266

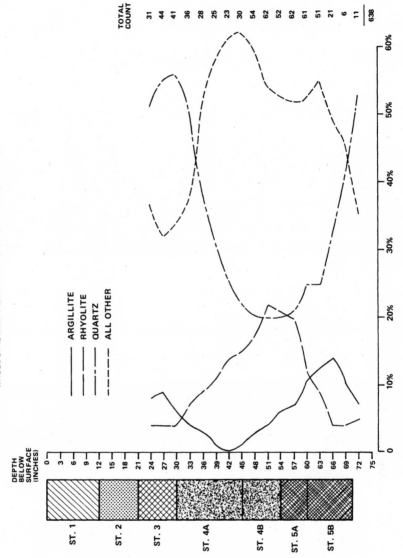

FIGURE 8   RAW MATERIAL FREQUENCY IN ARTIFACTS
WHOLE OR IDENTIFIABLE ARTIFACTS – CHIPPED STONE

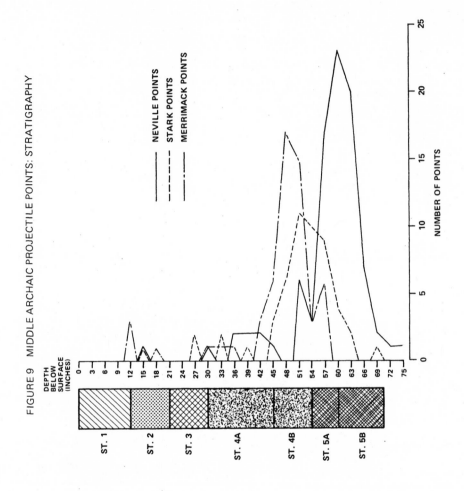

FIGURE 9 MIDDLE ARCHAIC PROJECTILE POINTS: STRATIGRAPHY

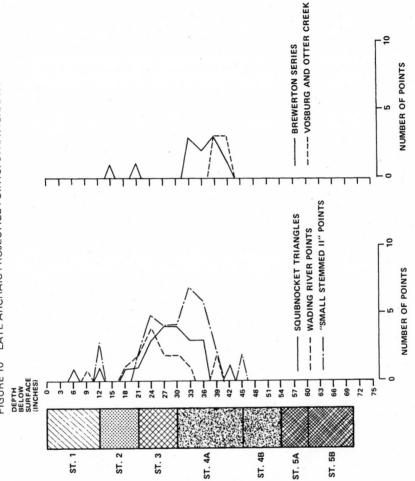

FIGURE 10   LATE ARCHAIC PROJECTILE POINTS: STRATIGRAPHY

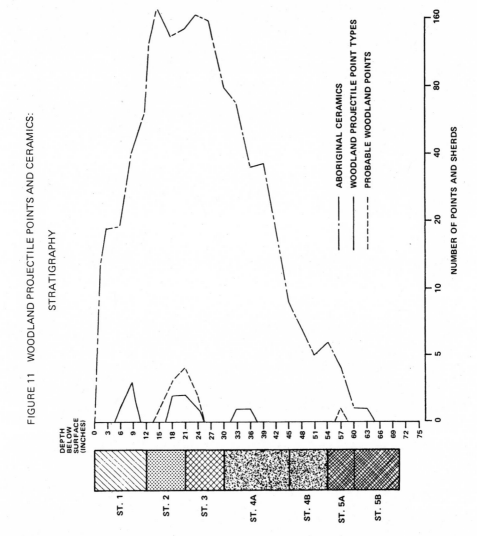

FIGURE 11   WOODLAND PROJECTILE POINTS AND CERAMICS: STRATIGRAPHY

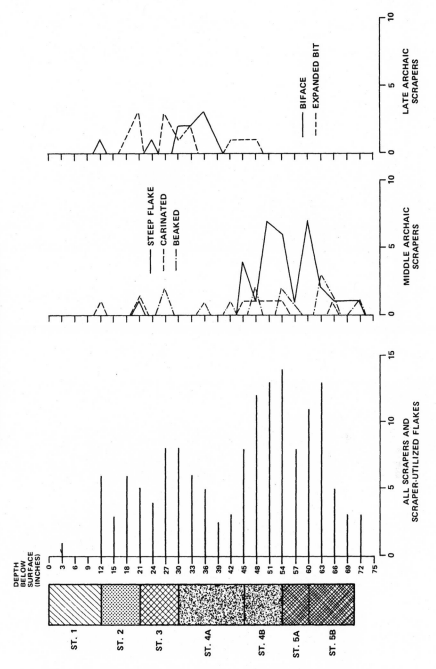

FIGURE 12   SCRAPERS: STRATIGRAPHY

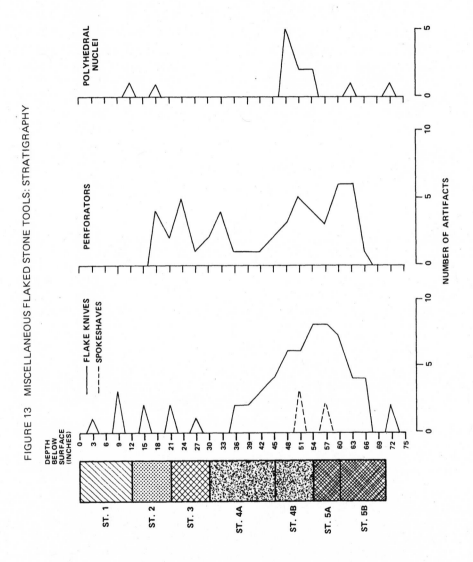

FIGURE 13   MISCELLANEOUS FLAKED STONE TOOLS: STRATIGRAPHY

3

Cultural Stratigraphy and Assemblages

The physical stratigraphy of the site which was described in chapter 1 is confirmed and complemented by stratigraphic relationships among many kinds of cultural debris. Brief descriptions of these classes of data will be presented before the discussion of the cultural assemblages which have been derived from them.

CULTURAL STRATIGRAPHY

The classes of cultural debris whose stratigraphic relationships are summarized below include: frequencies of lithic raw materials, selected chemical elements, frequencies of artifacts and features, distributions of major artifact types, and dated charcoal samples.

Lithic Materials Frequencies

The stratigraphic relevance of these data was first noticed by the excavators, who became aware of two frequency peaks of quartz chipping debris — one about one-third of the way down the stratigraphic column, the other near the base. The upper peak coincided with high frequencies of quartz artifacts; the lower peak did not appear to be reflected among the artifacts at those depths. Furthermore, the excavators noticed that a particular buff-colored rhyolite seemed to be restricted to low levels at the site, where it was very common.

Two major categories of lithic material were counted among the chipping debris in all squares, and a third category was tabulated during a recount of selected squares. These were: (1) quartz and quartzite, (2) buff rhyolite (see appendix), and (3) argillite (see appendix). The frequencies followed remarkably similar curves throughout the site, with the rhyolite peak between the two quartz peaks. Argillite proved to be a somewhat more variable, and minor, constituent of the debris. Together, these three rock types account for more than half of the chipping waste at the site. Other material, lumped together in figures 7

95

and 8, includes many different volcanic and metamorphic rocks and cryptocrystalline silicates.

Figure 7 summarizes the raw material frequencies in the chipping waste from square N3W1. This square was chosen to represent all thirty-four squares because the counting and identification were done with special care and accuracy and the stratigraphy was well controlled. The trends shown agree well with those of the other squares except for some exaggeration of the upper argillite peak in this instance. Chip counts were calculated as percentages of the total for each level below the plow zone; the percentages were then recalculated by the method of running averages (averaging adjacent units in sets of three) in order to smooth the curves for graphic presentation. The averaging suppresses minor oscillations on the trend lines without changing the shape of the major curves significantly.

Figure 8 is a graph, similarly constructed, showing trends in raw material frequencies of chipped stone artifacts from the entire excavated area. In general, the artifact trends agree well with the trends defined in the chipping waste. The unimodality of the rhyolite curve on both charts is notable. The rhyolite peak on figure 8 would have been significantly steeper if the broken rough bifaces had been counted. The quartz curve contradicts the excavators' observations of few quartz artifacts in the lowest levels. In fact, the low absolute numbers of artifacts included a high percentage of flake scrapers made of quartz, which were not recognized as artifacts in the field. The argillite peaks in Strata 3 and 5 agree with the trends in chipping waste reasonably well, with some shifts in the peak positions. The miscellany curve on the artifact graph is especially interesting in its failure to follow the dip in the flake trend in Stratum 4. Especially revealing is the peak in the lower part of Stratum 4A; artifacts of miscellaneous materials dominate there in levels where artifacts are relatively rare and where miscellaneous materials are not important in the chipping waste. A high proportion of artifacts of exotic materials, not made at the site, is indicated there. This conclusion is confirmed in the artifact assemblages to be reported below.

Microchemical Analysis

A series of samples was selected from the soil monolith at 6-inch intervals immediately above the sediment samples (fig. 6). These were submitted to the Microanalysis Laboratory at the University of Massachusetts by Peter Thomas of the Department of Anthropology, as part of an investigation into the chemistry of archaeological soils. Mr. Thomas comments as follows:

The interest in this case was to test, by several microchemical procedures, for higher than normal concentrations of iodine and mercury. The presence of these elements was hypothesized on the basis of the following assumptions: 1) A comparison of the total iodine content of mammals, fresh water and anadromous fish gives an approximate ratio of 1:1:10—3,428 mg/100 kg: 3-4,000 mg/100 kg: 34,000 mg/100 kg. Furthermore, it is unlikely that the butchering of large game or of fresh water fish would have increased the iodine content of the site soil to any marked degree. It is probable that much of the large game consumed at the Neville site was butchered in the field, where the carcass portion containing the largest amount of iodine, the thyroid, would have been abandoned. Additionally, fresh water fish species could simply not be caught in any numbers approaching those of salmon or shad.

2) Since it has been demonstrated that mercury compounds existed in ocean fish before modern pollutants became a factor (Hammond 1971:788), it was felt that mercury might follow similar trends, paralleling the increases or decreases of iodine in the column samples, thus helping to confirm an association of iodine and mercury with anadromous fish exploitation. As may be seen from the table (5), however, no such trend exists. Nevertheless, high mercury content in the profiles does tend to substantiate the hypothesis.

A midden is a geochemical anomaly which tends to depart from the norm of corresponding nonmidden soil profiles and horizons. In time and under favorable circumstances, these anomalies may weather to the extent that they approach the norm. The column profile for the Neville site, with less than .1 ppm iodine for the entire sequence, illustrates such a trend since the iodine occurs in the iodide form — an anion which is easily lost during chemical reactions in the soil. Except for level H, the mercury profile also appears to be indicative of a weathering out of these elements to a lower depth. Unlike iodine, Hg^{++} is a cation, and as such should be more tightly held in the exchange complex of the midden, usually bonded to clays or to charcoal. It is possible that signficant mercury increases in levels A-E and H, particularly the latter, do have some historical significance, since an increased exchange capacity at these levels may be at least partially attributed to occupation density. The .1 ppm level of Hg at the base of the 18th century plowzone illustrates the contrast to the midden deposits below. Mercury concentrations in the lower levels may also be due to the fact that clays, one of the bonding agents, have leached to these depths from above. The critical fact, however, is that mercury exists at all, and in such quantities. Its presence appears to be tied to anadromous fishing since no mammalian or floral species can be suggested as a source.

At the same time as the testing for iodine and mercury, concentrations of carbon, nitrogen, phosphorous, and calcium were measured. The results are presented in table 5.

As with the sediment analysis, the results raise many more questions than can be answered. The physical and chemical factors which influence the concentration of these elements in soils, especially ancient soils, are not well understood (Cook and Heizer 1965). In the present case, no archaeologically sterile soil from Amoskeag was available for contrast, and only the one series of stratified samples existed. Background values derived from nonagricultural and nonarchaeological

TABLE 5

VALUES OF SELECTED CHEMICAL ELEMENTS

Sample	Stratum	%C	%N	%P	%Ca	I ppm	Hg ppm
I	2/3	1.95	.136	.63	.0375	⟨.1	⟨.1
H	3	2.10	.113	.76	.0469	⟨.1	5.0
G	4A	1.60	.087	.67	.0174	⟨.1	.8
F	4A	1.09	.032	.63	.0241	⟨.1	.8
E	4B	1.04	.001	.42	.0241	⟨.1	3.0
D	4B	1.10	.030	.63	.0522	⟨.1	3.0
C	5	1.08	.026	.49	.0731	⟨.1	11.0
B	5	1.24	.001	.76	.0418	⟨.1	38.0
A	Subsoil/ 5B	.74	.023	.48	.0174	⟨.1	25.0

sandy loam in the middle Connecticut Valley have been supplied by Mr. Thomas, so that some tentative interpretations can be made.

In spite of the black color of most of the soil samples, the carbon concentration is relatively low. It is close to the values of the control samples, which had a range of .98 to 2.76%, with the mean at 1.94%. The control sample values reflect conditions near the surface in normal soil profiles. In nonmidden soils, the carbon concentration rapidly decreases below the uppermost soil horizons because of oxidation and leaching below the A zone. No such gradient has developed in the organically enriched midden soils of this site. The carbon values measured indicate a rather high prehistoric occupation density and delineate well the contrast between midden and subsoil at the base of the column, in Samples B and A.

Calcium leaches readily from mildly acid soils (Cook and Heizer 1965, p. 19); here, the concentrations vary so irregularly throughout the column, independently of the other elements, that no simple explanation for the calcium values is sufficient. Nitrogen values decline predictably and regularly from top to bottom, as a function of age, with two interesting but unexplained exceptions (Samples E and B). The phosphorous values, irregular as they are, indicate significant enrichment by organic wastes. Background values for phosphorous in sandy loam soils range from .04 to .09%, with the mean at .075%. The Neville soils are ten times richer in phosphorous. The low value for Sample E, lower even than Sample A from the subsoil, is notable.

The results of the microchemical analysis are interesting not only for their demonstration of artificial chemical enrichment throughout the soil column but also for their general conformity to stratigraphic subdivisions (fig. 6). The anomaly of Sample E is hard to explain; its organic constituents are very low, its mercury value moderate. Its true stratigraphic position may be the empty zone of lower 4A rather than the indicated upper 4B provenience. If 4B is the correct position, the sample was close to the occupation floor at 45 inches, and may have been subjected to heavier weathering due to slower sedimentation at that time.

Artifact Frequencies

The raw frequencies of all classifiable stone artifacts display a bimodal distribution with depth. Peaks occur near the 27- to 30-inch level in the lower part of Stratum 3 and in the 51- to 63-inch levels in lower 4B, 5A, and upper 5B. The lower peak is the larger and is bifurcated by a relatively low artifact count in the 54- to 57-inch level at the 4B/5A interface. These distributions are reflected in the counts of chipped stone artifacts in figure 8 and in the frequency calculations of table 6. They are assumed to be rough indicators of the intensities of site use through time. The peak locations must approximate the depths of major occupation floors, near 27, 51, and 57 to 63 inches.

TABLE 6

FREQUENCIES AND DENSITIES OF
CLASSIFIABLE STONE ARTIFACTS

Stratum	No. of Excava- tion Units*	No. of Artifacts	% Artifacts	Density (artifacts per exc. unit)
1	136	22	2	.16
2	102	73	8	.72
3	102	130	14	1.27
4A	170	201	21	1.18
4B	102	172	18	1.69
5A	68	131	15	1.94
5B	102	182	19	1.78
subsoil 69-75 in.	68	32	3	.47
Totals	850	943	100	—

*Excavation Unit = 5^2 ft. x 3 in. = 8.25 cu. ft.

34 squares; 25 3-in. levels per square

Table 6 is an attempt to define some parameters of site-use intensity and to compare vertical artifact distributions with the physical stratigraphic units. Artifact counts per arbitrary excavation level are the basic data for the table. The levels have been assigned to strata in accordance with the modal stratigraphic interface definitions displayed in figures 8 to 13. Obviously, the resultant totals for artifacts per stratum are gross approximations only, since excavation levels only rarely coincided with stratigraphic interfaces; an inherent error of 3 inches has been admitted already (chapter 1). The artifact percentages in table 6 are merely first approximations to intensity parameters, since their values are partly dependent upon the thickness of the several strata. The density figures more directly reflect the intensity of cultural debris per stratum, as they are corrected for volume. The significance of the correction is shown in the contrast between the percentage figure for Stratum 5A, which is lower than those above and below it, and the density index, which is relatively higher. It has not been possible to correct the density indexes for possibly different accumulation rates for the several strata; there are not enough radiocarbon dates to construct a reliable chronology for the interfaces.

The contrasts in the intensity indexes above and below the 4A/B interface are well demonstrated in table 6. The 6,000-year-old interface at 45 inches (4A/B), almost invisible in the physical stratigraphy, is the major cultural interface at the site. It separates Middle Archaic cultures from Late Archaic and later and marks a significant change in the intensity, and perhaps the purpose, of site use.

Feature Frequencies

Feature recording was poorly controlled during excavation. Only 47% of the squares had any reported features. Many of the features which were recorded extended across square boundaries; in only one case was the continuity reported. Therefore, the total of forty-five discrete features (two double-numbered) is a minimal count. The distribution presented on table 7 represents observation and recording conditions much more than prehistoric activities.

The dominance of features in Stratum 5B can be almost entirely accounted for by the intrusion of pits with black fill into the yellow subsoil beneath the lowest occupation floor. Twenty-seven of the twenty-nine features assigned to Stratum 5B were observed at or below the 69-inch level. The two exceptions are features which were associated with a floor at 66 inches in the W1 row of squares (see fig. 4, N3W1).

Feature 18 was recorded at the 5A/B interface and is left unassigned in table 7. Features 15 and 17 are very likely parts of a single scatter of hearth stones and charcoal; they were recorded separately at two successive levels of a single square (N5), in Stratum 5A. This stratum was generally darker in color than 5B; it is likely that many other features were missed during excavation. The discordance of radiocarbon ages and their stratigraphic relationships within Stratum 5 (table 8) is probably caused by extensive unobserved pitting.

Observation conditions were poor throughout Stratum 4, but a lighter colored lensing near the top of 4B allowed some crucial feature recogni-

TABLE 7

FEATURE DISTRIBUTIONS AND FREQUENCIES

Stratum	Features	No. of Features	% of Recorded Features
2	19, 28, 38, 41	4	9.0
3	2, 29, 30	3	6.8
4A	40?	1	2.2
4B	10, 14, 16, (20 + 37), 21, 36	6	13.6
5A	(15 + 17), 18?	1(2)	2.2
5B	18? 1, 3, 4, 5, 6, 7, 8, 9, 11, 12, 13, 22, 23, 24, 25, 26, 27, 31, 32, 33, 34, 35, 39, 42, 43, 44, 45, 46, 47	29(30)	65.9
Totals		44 + 1	99.7

tion there. All the 4B features except #16 were near the top of 4B, on or directly under the occupation floor. Feature 40 was recognized intruding into 4B from a higher level. No features directly associated with 4A activities were recorded. The dense black color of 4A made feature recognition nearly impossible in the field.

Stratum 3 was heavily intruded by features from Stratum 2, which did not show well as color contrasts. The extent of the disturbance can be approximated by observing the potsherd counts on figure 11. In many cases, the intrusive status of the sherds could be demonstrated by matching fragments of single vessels through successive levels from Stratum 2 to 3. The only feature recorded *in situ* in Stratum 3 was #29. Features 2 and 30 have a high probability of association with Stratum 3, although they were recorded in 4A.

The features assigned to Stratum 2 were all intrusive into Stratum 3 and truncated by the plow sole which defined the 2/3 interface. The plow zone itself retained no feature structures except for trenches intrusive from above the 1/2 interface, which are not considered here.

Artifact Type Distributions

The clustering of artifact types and classes by strata was one of the most satisfying results of this study. The vertical distributions of the major artifact groups are graphed in figures 9 to 13, where the coincidences with physical strata can be clearly seen. The graphs display the provenience of all artifacts of each class, including those known to be in disturbed contexts. This was done because not all disturbances could be demonstrated;

therefore, the graphed distributions show maximal dispersals. It is clear that in nearly all categories some displacement has occurred both upward and downward. The specimens represented in the discontinuous tails of several groups have clearly been disassociated mechanically from the distributional peaks. Consequently, the peaks of the several distributions are more significant than the tails. The decision to graph actual frequencies rather than percentage curves of the battleship form was made in order to stress the strength of the clustering tendencies and the isolation of many of the displaced pieces.

The projectile point distributions fall into three main groups: (1) the Middle Archaic points below the 4A/B interface (fig. 9), (2) the Late Archaic points in Strata 4A and 3 (fig. 10), and (3) the Woodland points in Stratum 2 (fig. 11). Within the Middle Archaic group, the three types succeed each other in a regular progression. Neville and Merrimack points have nearly mutually exclusive distributions, with the boundary near the 5A/4B interface. Stark points are associated with both of the other types; it is not clear whether they represent an intermediate form or a temporal overlap of an independent type. Among the Late Archaic points graphed, the Brewerton, Vosburg , and Otter Creek types stand apart stratigraphically as well as typologically. Minor Late Archaic point types and Woodland types will be discussed below in the section on "Assemblages."

The importance of the 4A/B interface for the cultural stratigraphy is manifest also on figures 12 and 13, where it separates Middle Archaic scraper types from later ones, marks the effective limit of flake knives, spokeshaves, and polyhedral nuclei and subdivides the perforator distribution. A secondary cultural break, between 54 and 57 inches near the 4B/5A interface, is also evident on those two figures, confirming the Neville:Merrimack boundary on figure 9.

The distribution of aboriginal ceramics is shown on figure 11 by a special scale on which each interval represents twice as many units as the interval to its left. The rapid decline below Stratum 2 is almost symmetrical with that above. The role of physical displacement is the same in each case.

Dated Charcoal Samples

A dozen charcoal samples from the site were analyzed at Geochron Laboratories. The results are shown on table 8. Four of the ages are irreconcilable with their recorded stratigraphic positions. The other eight are acceptable and useful, although less orderly than might be desired.

The four samples over 7,000 years old came from Stratum 5, in fascinating disarray. They agree sufficiently well to date Stratum 5 and all its contents to the eighth millennium B.P. Two other samples in equivalent stratigraphic situations are much younger.

Sample 2531 is one of two from square N2E2, both of which are anomalous, for reasons unknown. Sample 1320, 5,385±380 years old, was the first sample submitted from the site. It was selected for its basal position and its association with a Neville point, although "the final recovery of purified charcoal was not quite as large as I would have initially expected" (letter to P. McLane from Geochron, 6/7/68). Its situation near but lower than sample 1747, which is 2,265 radiocarbon years older, makes it highly suspect; it may be from a rodent burrow.

Two of the six samples from above Stratum 5 appear to be out of place (1920, 2529). They are both from depths near 36 inches and from adjacent squares. They were selected in hopes of dating the Brewerton points nearby, but they are too young by a millennium or more. They are also younger than Sample 1749, which was stratigraphically higher and quite congruent with its Squibnocket comples associations.

TABLE 8
RADIOCARBON AGES AND SAMPLE PROVENIENCES

Lab No.	Age B.P.*	Square	Fea-ture	Depth	Stratum	Comment
GX 2530	395±90	N6	19	28"	3	intrusive from St. 2
2529	3025±185	N2E2	30	36"	4A	?
1920	3445±130	N1E2	--	36-39"	4A	?
1749	4390±180	N3E1	--	33-36"	4A	
2531	4715±240	N2E2	--	57-60"	5A	small sample; possibly contaminated
1320	5385±380	N5	--	72-75"	subsoil	small sample; below 1746, 1747
1748	5910±180	N4	10	45-48"	4A/B	
1921	6060±130	N1E2	--	42-45"	4A/B	
1449	7015±160	N1E2	23	69-75"	5B/ subsoil	
1922	7210±140	N4	--	54-57"	4B/5A	
1747	7650±400	N5	11	69-72"	5B	
1746	7740±280	N5	17	54-57"	5A	above 1747

*half-life value 5570; before AD 1950

The age of the latter sample is fully acceptable for its position in upper 4A. Samples 1921 and 1748, closely contemporary, fix the age of the 4A/B interface at about 6,000 years ago. Sample 2530 was recorded as coming from a hearth *in situ* in Stratum 3; its association with pot-sherds in intrusive Feature 19 was recognized only later, when the feature inventory was completed. The age is acceptable for a Woodland period feature; unfortunately, the sherds are tiny and nondescript.

The dated samples, therefore, give four solid control points which can help to date the strata. Stratum 5 is older than 7,015±160 radio-carbon years, with a maximum age of at least 7,740±280 years. The 4A/B interface is about 6,000 years old. The upper part of Stratum 4A, just below the 3/4A interface, is 4,390±180 years old, and one feature in Stratum 2 is 395±90 years old. Other chronological control points can be defined from cultural data; they will be discussed below and in chapter 4.

ASSEMBLAGES

The contents of Strata 5B through 2 will be summarized below. The intention is to describe successive assemblages of artifacts, including features, using stratigraphic subdivisions as the units of analysis. This approach gives good results for Strata 5B, 5A, and 4B. In Strata 4A and 3, however, it is necessary to further subdivide the stratigraphic units in order to isolate discrete cultural assemblages which can be recognized at the level of excavation unit (3-inch level) analysis. In Stratum 2, the plow zone mixing has destroyed all vertical distinctions, so that cultural units can be discerned only on the basis of typological units defined elsewhere.

It is not possible to quantify the results of this summary with any precision. The stratigraphic interfaces are defined only approximately, and it is known that stratigraphic disturbances were not dependably re-corded. Because of these complications, it was decided to limit statis-tical manipulations to a minimum, to avoid a spurious appearance of ac-curacy. Frequencies of artifact classes will be compared only within units, as ratios of projectile points to other classes (table 9). The total numbers of artifacts per unit which will be discussed will usually be somewhat lower than the totals given on table 6, because items con-sidered to be displaced will not be included in the summaries. In addi-tion to items known to be from intrusive features, displaced artifacts include all those in the tails of distribution curves (figs. 9 to 13) which are separated from the body of the curve by a gap of 3 inches or more.

Stratum 5B

Only four kinds of projectile points are distinguished here: the Neville

type (54), the Neville variant (3), the Stark type (7), and the one bifur-
cate base point (pl. 6d). In addition, eight bifaces too incomplete or
idiosyncratic for typing were recognized as projectile points. Artifacts
interpreted as scrapers include steep flake scrapers (12), beaked scrapers (5), quartz crystal scrapers (2), early flake end scrapers (3)
(pl.7j-l), miscellaneous and casual flake scrapers (13). There were thirteen perforators, which are either simple shaft perforators or have
Neville style bases. Flake knives (17), one spokeshave, and two polyhedral nuclei of quartz crystal complete the inventory of classified
chipped stone tools. The ratios of projectile points to other major
classes of artifacts are presented on table 9. Large biface fragments,
present but not counted, included the fine piece illustrated on plate
6f. The earliest rhyolite workshop concentration occurred at 63 inches
in square N8.

Ground stone tools are represented by fragments only; the presence
of any ground stone at this level is notable. There were two fragments
of winged atlatl weights, two pieces of ground slate, and a pecked and
ground poll of an adze or gouge. Five tabular abraders indicate the
grinding of other materials against stone, as does one small hone/
whetstone. These small scraps cannot be taken as proof of ground stone
tools in the 5B assemblage; they can, however, give notice that the possibility exists, and should be tested elsewhere.

Rough stone tools include two of the uninterpreted Middle Archaic
friable cylinders. Heavy flaked choppers occur in three forms — a con-
vex-bitted biface, a pick (pl. 17a), and a core chopper. There were fourteen hammers, including six pebble hammers, two core hammers, and
six angular cobble hammers. An equal number (14) of unutilized cobbles (8) and pebbles (6) were recovered from this stratum. Three slabs
of abrasive stone, not obviously used, were intentionally brought to
the site.

Except for the rhyolite workshop, which was bagged as a unit, associations of artifacts were not recorded more closely than by excavation
unit (5' x 5' x 3"). Few significant relationships emerge from examination of the gross spatial distributions. The two friable cylinders were in
square N8E1, separated by one full excavation unit; they could have
been together in a pit. The ground slate pieces were in adjacent squares
at 63 to 66 inches. The crystal scrapers were in adjacent squares at successive levels near the top of 5B. Unmodified pebbles occurred within
one square or excavation unit of pebble hammers in three instances.
Five of the large hammers were at or below the base of the occupation,
probably in shallow pits; in two cases they were so recorded.

The raw materials used for chipped stone tools in Stratum 5B were
highly diversified. The relatively heavy use of quartz and quartzite has
been reported previously. Some of the assorted volcanic stones observed in artifacts and debitage from this stratum are visually com-

parable to materials from northeastern Massachusetts with which I am familiar. Some of the andesite porphyries are very close to the Marble-head-Wakefield porphyries of Massachusetts (Dincauze 1968, p. 93), and some pieces of red indurated siltstone are indistinguishable in the hand from Saugus (Massachusetts) jasper. My inexperience with New Hampshire rocks reduces the reliability of these observations. The rhyolite workshop in upper 5B initiates the intensive utilization of that New Hampshire stone (see appendix), which is characteristic of the two strata above.

　　Five kinds of cultural features were recognized; they are described in chapter 2. Pits with charcoal and no stones were predominant; eighteen were recorded (table 7, with exceptions detailed below). There were five postholes, of which four, of questionable authenticity (Features 3 to 7), were in square N3. The unequivocal example, Feature 22, is illustrated on plate 2b. Two pits with hammerstones, Features 23 and 35, may be members of a larger class, since three other hammerstones were recovered at or below the basal occupation floor, where they may have been in pits. Feature 45, charcoal with scattered stones, and Feature 46, a charcoal concentration without a pit, complete the inventory.

TABLE 9

RATIOS OF PROJECTILE POINTS TO OTHER ARTIFACTS

Strata 5B, 5A, and 4B

Points:	5B	5A	4B
: scrapers	2:1	2.4:1	2:1
: flake knives	4:1	3.5:1	4.5:1
: perforators	5.5:1	8:1	9.2:1
: hammers	5:1	18:1	12:1

　　Two radiocarbon dates from this stratum were associated with features (table 8). Feature 11, a pit with charcoal fill, was 7,650±400 years old. Feature 23, a pit with a hammerstone, was 7,015±160 years old. The pits intruded the subsoil, where they were first recognized; their levels of origin were not observed. It is possible that neither sample is coeval with Stratum 5B, which could be somewhat older. The range from 7,015 to 7,650 is in good agreement with the estimated age of Coe's Stanly points, the close relatives of Neville points (Coe 1964, p. 54).

　　There is some evidence, in profiles and artifact frequencies by level, for the presence of two main occupation floors in this stratum. The lower was between 66 and 69 inches, the higher between 60 and 63 inches. The majority of the recorded features were in the southern part of the excavated area, south of square N6 (fig. 2). The lowest excavation

units, 66 to 72 inches, have almost all their artifacts south of square
N9, with one point in N26W3. Higher excavation units have artifacts
successively farther north, reaching N14 by 60 inches. The occupied
area was expanding or shifting to the north throughout the period of
accumulation of Stratum 5B.

Stratum 5A

The assemblage from 5A differs in subtle ways from that of 5B. It is
hard to assess the significance of the differences because of the stratigraphic uncertainties involved in the interface definitions. These uncertainties necessarily dominate efforts to understand 5A, which is the
shallowest stratigraphic unit at the site as well as the one with the highest artifact density index (table 6).

Neville and Stark projectile points occur in essentially equal numbers
(20 and 19, respectively); however, the former declines in frequency
throughout the stratum, while the latter increases (fig. 9). Additionally,
there are two Neville variant points, nine Merrimacks, and six untypable projectile points. Twenty-three scrapers include seven steep flake
scrapers of which two have noses, two quartz crystal scrapers, three
beaked scrapers, and eleven casual and miscellaneous flake scrapers.
Seven perforators include three with flake bases; the rest are unclassi-
fiable shaft fragments. Sixteen flake knives and two spokeshaves complete the chipped stone artifact counts (see table 9 for ratios). Large,
unfinished bifaces were numerous but not counted.

There is very little ground stone in this stratum — no ground slate,
no atlatl weight fragments, no abraders or whetstones. The outstanding exception is the full-grooved diorite axe from square N4, which
rested on the 5A/B interface at 60 inches and was first observed at 54
inches (pl. 15a).

The rough stone inventory reflects that of 5B, including one friable
cylinder, three choppers, one pebble hammer, and two core hammers.
No cobble hammers were reported. There were three cobbles and six
pebbles lacking any use-wear.

The small, calcined fragment of incised bone came from this stratum at 57 inches in square N1E3 (pl. 18b).

Associations of artifacts within excavation units were not demon-
strably significant; a few spatial groupings deserve comment. The quartz
crystal scrapers were in extreme southern squares, close to the similar
specimens in 5B. Rhyolite chipping debris representing a workshop area
was in square N2E1 at 57 to 60 inches, near two Neville points and a
crystal scraper. The three choppers were in central squares, N6, N9,
and N10. The incised bone fragment was not associated closely with
any classifiable stone artifact. The full-grooved axe, which crossed two
excavation units (54 to 60 inches), was surrounded by three Stark points,

two Merrimacks, and two Nevilles, as well as other typical Middle Archaic flake tools and a pebble hammer.

The frequency of quartz continued to decline among both the debitage and artifacts of this stratum (figs. 7 and 8). It was replaced by a rapid increase in the use of buff-colored rhyolite. The rhyolite dominance accounts for the relative decline in the frequencies of other materials, which reach their highest actual numbers in 5A and lower 4B.

Feature recognition was minimal in 5A. Feature 18 was at the 5A/B interface and may be related to either stratum. It was a pit with charcoal. Feature 15 + 17 was a scatter of granite and schist hearth stones with charcoal in square N5, in two successive levels. A charcoal sample saved from the upper level, 54 to 57 inches, was submitted for dating. A steep flake scraper, a flake knife, and a Merrimack point came from the two excavation units.

Three radiocarbon ages were determined for charcoal samples taken from this stratum (table 8). The sample from Feature 17 was 7,740± 280 years old; a sample collected at the same level in an adjacent square was 7,210±140 years old, and a sample collected 3 inches deeper a few feet to the south was 4,715±240 years old. The latter almost certainly does not date Stratum 5A. The relationships between the ages of the older two samples and that of the stratum remain unclarified. Each is within the error margin of one of the samples from Stratum 5B, so that there is no demonstrable difference between the radiocarbon ages of Strata 5A and 5B. Clearly, the latter is older, but by how much, and in what time range, is unknown.

Vertical distributions of artifacts indicate a floor near 57 inches. Artifacts in this stratum were more numerous in squares south of N4 than north of it, although they extended north to N26W3. None were recovered in N11 and N12.

Stratum 4B

The projectile point types are the same as in 5A, but their relative representations change. Nevilles (7) and Neville variants (3) are definitely minority types. Starks are about as numerous as in 5A (20). Merrimack points dominate the stratum, their numbers (38) being greater than all others combined. A unique tanged biface of more than passing interest was recovered in this stratum but probably is not coeval with the other artifacts (pl. 8a). It is a large piece, with steeply beveled edges, which has its closest correspondences among Kirk-related, stemmed bifaces of the Early Archaic south of New England (Ritchie and Funk 1971, Fig. 3#6; Coe 1964, Fig. 60). It seems out of place in its context of recovery, which was the 4A/B interface. Four untypable projectile points complete the count. Among the scrapers, the old steep-bitted flake scrapers (12) and beaked scrapers (3) are present; there are no quartz crystal scrapers. Carinated (4) and thick end scrapers (5) make their only significant appearance in this stratum. Miscellaneous (3) and casual flake scrapers (7) continue to be important numerically, as do flake knives (16). Spokeshaves reach their peak with three specimens in this stratum. Eight perforators include one simple shaft form and two with "Stark" style bases (pl. 4m) from the lowest part of the stratum and an unspecialized biface form from near the top. Artifact ratios are on table 9. The enigmatic polyhedral nuclei, with their occasional scraperlike noses, are indigenous to this stratum, where seven were recovered. Large unfinished bifaces were present.

Ground stone artifacts appear again, in numbers sufficient to inspire confidence in their presence. Parts of four separate winged atlatl weights were recovered within the stratum, including the "Stanly" specimen illustrated in plate 14c. At the 4A/B interface lay the small unfinished weight. The grooved axe blank from square N3W1 (pl. 15b) was in this stratum. Two fragments of ground slate were also found widely separated, and one tabular abrader.

Rough stone tools include some familiar older classes and some new ones. There was one chopper, the last of the friable cylinders, three core hammers, two angular cobble hammers, three unutilized cobbles, and one unworn pebble. A discoid cobble hammer may belong in this stratum or be intrusive from above where they are more numerous. On the uppermost occupation surface, at the 4A/B interface, lay the two full-grooved pebbles (pl. 16e).

In this stratum, the significant associations seem to be the vertical ones. The lower level shares more traits with Stratum 5A than do the upper ones. The new scraper types and the grooved pebbles appear in the upper levels, where the Merrimack points dominate. The spatial distributions are relatively uninformative about task sets. Five of the seven polyhedral nuclei occur in excavation units where scrapers are also present, but three types of scrapers are involved — two steep-bitted, two carinated, and one thick end scraper. Scrapers may occur singly or in groups; in the latter case, the specimens grouped are rarely of the same type.

Buff rhyolite dominates the flaking waste in this stratum and is important among the artifacts, although it declines in actual numbers. Other felsitic stones were apparently preferred over the rhyolite, or were more readily available. Especially common was a medium-gray porphyritic felsite, which was used for many Merrimack points. The chip counts begin to decline toward the top of 4B, indicating a reduced chipping industry, at least within the excavated area.

The features were mostly observed in the lighter colored lensing at the top of 4B, near the interface. They include charcoal without a pit (Feature 10) in square N4, for which a radiocarbon age was calculated, a cobble arrangement with charcoal in squares N5 and N6 (Feature 14; pl. 2a), a pit which extended from 45 inches in square N12 into underlying Stratum 5A (Feature 20 + 37), and two other concentrations of charcoal without obvious pits in the latter square (Features 21 and 36). A small concentration of calcined bone fragments (Feature 16) was found at 51 to 54 inches in square N5.

The dates from 4B come from the upper interface, close to 45 inches below the 1968 surface (table 8). The close agreement between the two samples and the congruence of the ages with their stratigraphic position is gratifying. The age of 6,000 years for the 4A/B interface provides a firm *terminus ante quem* for everything below it and a solid foundation from which to evaluate the stratigraphy above.

Artifact distributions indicate two probable living floors within the stratum. The major one was near 51 inches, the lesser near the upper interface. On the lower floor, artifact densities were highest south of square N9; only a few scattered pieces extended as far as N26W3. In the upper level there were fewer artifacts per excavation unit, and they were spread thinly over the area north to N15W2.

Stratum 4A

Immediately above the 4A/B interface there was a sharp reduction in the frequency of artifacts and debitage, a rise in the diversity of artifacts, and an increase in the familiarity of the artifact styles encountered. Major artifact trends are summarized on figures 10, 12, and 13. Stratum 4A corresponded to the base of the known cultural sequence of southern New England as that had been established by 1968 (Ritchie 1969b, Chapter VIII). It also included a relatively large amount of aboriginal ceramics (fig. 11). The detailed analysis which demonstrated the intrusive origin of the ceramics forced the conclusion that Stratum 4A had been subjected to a damaging amount of disturbance by pitting. As a result, the cultural stratigraphy is less crisply informative than might be desired.

The stratum will be subdivided into two zones for discussion of the cultural assemblages. The lower zone includes two excavation units, from 39 to 45 inches below the sod. The upper zone includes the highest two excavation units, from 30 to 36 inches. The unit between the zones (36 to 39 inches) will be summarized in relationship to those above and below. There is some support for this subdivision in the physical stratigraphy (fig. 4, N2E2 profile), and a great deal in the cultural stratigraphy.

Lower Zone

Eight of the thirty-four excavated squares had no artifacts in the lowest 3 inches of Stratum 4A, and counts were low elsewhere. The few projectile points in the lowest 6 inches of the stratum were early Late Archaic styles: three small points identified as Squibnocket (1) and Beekman triangles (2), two tentatively identified Wading River points, two small stemmed II points (pl. 11i), one Vosburg (pl. 9l) and two similar basal fragments, two Otter Creek points (pl. 9m, n) and a similar basal fragment, three Brewerton Side-Notched points, one Brewerton Eared-Notched (pl. 9o) and a similar corroded base (Ritchie 1971). In addition, there were four untypable points, two which were vaguely triangular and two stemmed. The Otter Creek, Vosburg, and Brewerton Side-Notched points occur nowhere else in the site; the other styles are more numerous at higher levels and may be intrusive here. It is not possible to tell, in the disturbed context of Stratum 4A, whether these few artifacts were actually coeval or not.

A suite of other items which are important only in this zone probably were associated with the Vosburg, Otter Creek, and Brewerton Side-Notched points. These include a tabular abrading stone, two fragments of heavy, ground stone tools, two convex-bladed slate knives (pl. 14a), graphite and yellow ocher and a paint-grinding slab, discoid and angular cobble hammers, and a notched pebble (pl. 16d).

The horizontal distributions of the items listed above are interesting, in further subdividing the associations. There is a major cluster of artifacts in and between squares N9 and N6, which includes the Vosburg and Otter Creek points, a Brewerton Side-Notched point, and one slate knife. Two Brewerton points and a Vosburg-like base are south of N4, with the rest of the ground stone pieces, the pigments, and the paint-grinding stone. One Brewerton Side-Notched point was alone in N26W3; a similar point was in the level above it (36 to 39 inches) in N26W2.

The small numbers of artifacts and amounts of chipping debris are highly diversified in terms of raw materials. Rhyolite drops from its peak representations; quartz begins to increase; and there is a significant jump in the numbers of artifacts made of unique materials. Chert artifacts and flakes increase in frequency, for the first time.

Feature 40, a pit with charcoal, was close to the bottom interface of 4A in square N8E1. Its provenience between 4A and 4B is in doubt, and no charcoal was saved. Feature recognition was extremely difficult in these levels. Even the limits of large Anglo-American trenches, which occasionally reached these depths, were ill recorded here.

No charcoal samples from these levels were submitted for dating because of small sample sizes, lack of associations, and uncertain feature provenience. Ages of 5,000 or more years are likely for the Otter Creek (Funk and Hoagland 1972, p. 12) and Vosburg points (Kinsey 1972, p. 398), at least. Efforts to date the Brewerton points with samples collected at the 36-inch level produced disappointing results (see table 8).

Upper Zone

Above 39 inches, Brewerton styles of projectile points are numerically insignificant. There are three Brewerton Eared-Notched points (pl. 9h, i) and one Eared-Triangle, all below 33 inches. They are in the southern squares, near their relatives in the lower zone, but they have no obvious associations beyond each other. The predominant projectile point styles in Upper 4A are the stemmed and triangular styles of the small point or narrow point tradition of the southern New England Late Archaic (Ritchie 1971, pp. 121, 126, 127, 131). The frequencies and distributions of Squibnocket Triangles (pl. 10a, e, f, h), small stemmed II points (pl. 11a, b, d, g, h, k, m, n), and Wading River points (pl. 10n, q) are summarized in figure 10. In addition, there were four possible Beekman triangles (pl. 10c, j, k) and ten untypable points which include a corroded side-notched piece, three triangles in the uppermost level, and an assortment of stemmed points, mostly small. One well-made stemmed point (pl. 9d) from 33 to 36 inches may be related to Late Archaic points of coastal Maine. Three small notched triangles (pl. 9j) were in the upper zone.

Figure 12 displays the change in scraper styles which occurred above the 4A/B interface. The biface and expanded bit scrapers appear to be normal associates of the small stemmed and triangular projectile points at this site. Three angled scrapers are present with them. Four Late Archaic miscellaneous scrapers are discussed in chapter 2, where the possible association of two flake scrapers with Brewerton points is mentioned. Casual flake tools are so rare in these levels that it is difficult to know whether or not they are intrusive. Perforators become numerous and interesting in the upper zone (fig. 13) but, again, some may be intrusive. There are three perforators with biface bases (pl. 13i, k), two shaft fragments, and a simple shaft perforator which may have been used to ream hafting sockets for small stemmed points (pls. 13h and 23a).

Ground stone tools include blade fragments of two gouges (pl. 14g) and a third fragment which could be from either a gouge or an adze. Only one centrum fragment of an atlatl weight was recovered. There was a tantalizingly small fragment of a comb-back ulu in the upper level of square N1E2, which may be displaced, and an unidentifiable fragment of ground slate from N7E1. The only rough stone tools in the upper zone were three hammers, one each of the core, angular cobble, and discoid cobble classes.

Beyond the obvious stratigraphic associations among the projectile point and scraper styles which characterize this zone (figs. 10 and 12), little can be said about tool kits. No informative spatial distributions were recognized.

This zone evidences the rise of quartz use to its second and major peak at the 4A/3 interface. Rhyolite has effectively gone out of use; its continued representation is probably due to disturbance of lower levels by pit digging. The use of materials other than quartz and argillite declines.

In spite of the abundant evidence of the results of pitting from and into this zone, no features were recognized in the greasy black matrix.

Poor conditions for feature recognition are almost certainly sufficient explanation for the scatter of radiocarbon ages in this zone (table 8, Samples 2529, 1920, and 1749). Of the three, Sample 1749 is by far the most acceptable. It falls within the range of radiocarbon ages elsewhere associated with small stemmed and triangular projectile points (Dincauze 1973, p. 31), and it is consistent with both its natural and cultural stratigraphic relationships. In spite of the fact that there is no evidence in the site records, Samples 2529 and 1920, with their fourth millennium dates, may have been intruded into Stratum 4A from Strata 3 or 2, where artifacts of the appropriate ages were recovered.

Stratum 3

Stratum 3, like 4A, is best discussed in two parts: a lower zone encompassing the two excavation levels between 24 and 30 inches; and an upper zone from 21 to 24 inches. This division makes possible a more lucid discussion of the artifact distributions. It has no other independent justification.

Lower Zone

These levels contain relics of two distinct cultural traditions of the southern New England Late Archaic. They can only be separated on the basis of assemblages demonstrated elsewhere. The small point/narrow point tradition (Ritchie 1969a, p. 144) is represented by eight Squibnocket triangles, three Beekman triangles, six Wading River stemmed, one Squibnocket stemmed, and ten small stemmed II projectile points (pls. 10b, d, g, l, m, o, p and 11e, f, j, o; fig. 10), and probably by three expanded-bit scrapers (fig. 12). An additional twelve untypable small stemmed points and fragments and two roughly triangular small points are probably related to the above.

The Susquehanna/Broadspear tradition is represented by artifacts typical of the Atlantic phase (Dincauze 1972). An Atlantic knife of black indurated siltstone or dull chert was recovered point down at the base of Stratum 3 in square N10 (pl. 9a). Nearby, in N11, was a spearpoint of rhyolite porphyry (pl. 9e). A basal fragment of a third Atlantic implement blade was recovered in the same stratigraphic position in N26W2. Four ovoid biface scrapers, like the one illustrated on pl. 9b, were at the other end of the excavated area, in the N3-N1 rows of squares. In the same area was the wing fragment of an atlatl weight of the faceted-edge style typical of Atlantic contexts.

A miscellaneous assortment of Late Archaic artifacts from this zone cannot be confidently associated with either tradition to the exclusion of the other. A stemmed point (pl. 9c) may even be intrusive here, or a product of the Maine Archaic. Four scrapers shaped on spalls, two trimmed flake knives unlike the Middle Archaic style, a perforator on a flake, and two biface-based perforators and four perforator shaft fragments are too amorphous to be recognized as the products of a particular cultural tradition. Two scraps of ground slate, two possible bone fragments, two angular cobble hammers, a broken strike-a-light, and a few lumps of graphite complete the inventory.

Raw material patterns cannot be discussed responsibly in isolation from Stratum 2, because of the extensive pitting into these levels from above. Figures 7 and 8 show the major trends in the lower zone of Stratum 3. Above that, through Stratum 2, the directions of the quartz and other materials curves do not change; quartz continues to decline and miscellany to increase in frequency. Among the miscellaneous materials represented, felsites are most important; there is also a signficantly strong showing of various cryptocrystalline silicates — chalcedonies, jaspers, and cherts — in Stratum 2 and the upper zone of Stratum 3.

The base of Stratum 3 in N3 was especially black in color, with a few large pieces of charcoal visible among a scatter of eight granite and schist stones. These observations were dignified as Feature 2. There were no artifact associations. A second feature (#29) from the same position in N2E1 was a "Black charcoal fire area" in the southeast corner of the square. There were no artifacts in the excavation unit where it was recognized. Feature 30, which was recorded in Stratum 4A, may have originated in either 3 or 2, where its age would be less anomalous. Features 19, 28, 38, and 41 were recorded in Stratum 3, but were intrusive from Stratum 2.

There are no radiocarbon ages directly applicable to Stratum 3. The age of 4,390±180 in the upper zone of Stratum 4 suggests a beginning for Stratum 3 around 4,000 years ago. The Atlantic artifacts in the lower zone of 3 are at least 3,600 years old, and probably older (Dincauze 1972, p. 56). The triangular and small stemmed points are elsewhere about 4,000 years old (Ritchie 1969b, p. 231). Good boundary dates have not been secured for the small point tradition; we do not know the extremes of its temporal range.

The lower zone of Stratum 3 probably encloses an occupation floor close to the 27-inch level, where artifact frequencies were highest. Very few artifacts were recovered north of square N12.

Upper Zone

Very little can be said about the 21- to 24-inch excavation unit except that it is a very mixed bag. In places, it may be the base of Stratum 2 (N3W1, N5, N7E1, N8, N10), but in most squares for which there is information it is the upper part of Stratum 3. The mixture of Late Archaic and Woodland artifacts which occurs here can be appreciated by comparing figure 11 with figures 10 and 12. In addition to the mixture of cultural periods, the level has a relatively low artifact count; classifiable stone artifacts were recovered from only sixteen squares. The representation of major artifact types can be read from the graphs. The Woodland points at this level include a Levanna point, a Rossville, and the probable Woodland artifacts illustrated on plate 12c, g, l. Three expanded-bit scrapers (pls. 13e and 23h) and a scatter of odds and ends complete the meager chipped tool inventory. A small hammerstone of pink granite and the ovoid atlatl weight fragment are the only notable heavy stone tools (pl. 14b). The pottery here belongs to no distinct period or style; rather, it includes a little bit of everything — some of it known to be in pits, all of it intruded from upper levels. There were no classifiable stone artifacts north of N11.

The discussion of raw materials, features, and dates for the lower zone of Stratum 3 applies to this part also, since there are no independent data on any of these phenomena from the upper zone.

Stratum 2

The plow zone of Stratum 2 had its upper limits above 15 inches and its lower limits between 21 and 24 inches. The plow churning obliterated all stratigraphic relationships and features from those levels and mixed seventeenth-, eighteenth-, and nineteenth-century Anglo-American artifacts with aboriginal relics up to 3,400 years older. Plowing broke and scattered ancient ceramic vessels and exposed to view objects buried centuries before by wind-transported sand. Attractive, curious, or obvious artifacts were probably pocketed by the plowmen and others over the decades. The overturned soil was oxidized, subjected to intensified leaching, and chemically depleted by agriculture (table 5). Buried in 1835-42, it preserved only an impoverished record of its original contents, plus a small accumulation of trash from farm and farmhouse.

The content of major artifact types is shown on figures 9-13. In addition, there was one Brewerton Eared-Notched point of felsite, a Normanskill point of gray chert (pl. 9k), and a Wayland Notched point (pl. 9f) among the Late Archaic types represented (Ritchie 1971; Dincauze 1968, p. 23). Among the Early and Middle Woodland points from Stratum 2 are those illustrated on plate 12d, h, and j. Of two bifacial Meadowood scrapers (pl. 13o, p) one was made of Deepkill chert (pl. 13o) as was a small flake scraper (pl. 13n). Three long-flake end scrapers (pls. 13m and 23i) occur nowhere else at the site, so must be considered *in situ* in Stratum 2. Among seven trimmed and utilized flakes were two each of Deepkill chert and of yellow jasper.

A unique ground slate pendant was recovered partly from Stratum 2 (pl. 14d); other parts of it were at 27 inches in an adjacent square. The simplest explanation is that the plow truncated a pit in which the fragments had been buried. Very few heavy stone tools were present, perhaps because of their high visibility in a plow zone. A medial fragment of a gouge, a tabular abrader, and an angular cobble hammer comprise the lot.

Artifacts of European and Anglo-American manufacture found at the site have not been studied in detail. Their inadvertent exclusion from the artifacts shipped to Buffalo prevented any detailed analysis and precluded their illustration for this report. A preliminary study of the artifacts sealed under Stratum 1 was made by R. M. Gramly in 1972. The only artifacts of seventeenth-century age are fragments of three pipes and half a round glass bead. The pipes are all dated before 1680 on the basis of bowl form or stem bore (9/64 in. and 8/64 in.). Two of the pipes were made of red-buff clay in early- to mid-seventeenth-century forms; the third was of white clay with a rouletted rim. These artifacts are quintessential trade objects. It is very likely that they were brought to Amoskeag by Indian owners in the seventeenth century. There is no evidence for any further activity at the site until nearly the middle of the eighteenth century; that is, until after the settlement of Archibald Stark in 1736. A very few artifacts made in the last half of the eighteenth century were identified in the debris. These include a sherd of Jackfield ware, shell-edged creamware, and bead-and-reel creamware. Lead-glazed red earthenware sherds cannot be dated closely enough to assign between the eighteenth and nineteenth centuries. John Stark's military interests seem to be reflected in the presence of two French gunflints, lead bullets, and lead spillage. Nineteenth-century articles were far more abundant and diverse than immediately older ones, even though the stratum was sealed off by 1842. The nineteenth-century materials include, but are not limited to, cut nails, a glass inkwell with pontil mark, pressed lead and soda glass, transfer printed pearlware and creamware, spongeware, Albany slipped stoneware, buttons, and bricks (Cotter 1968; Hume 1970). The construction activity at the site between 1839 and 1842 is represented by two hallmarks — a railroad spike and a coin of 1841.

The lithic raw materials of Stratum 2 were summarized above, in the discussion of Stratum 3. The presence of jasper and chert artifacts and chips in unprecedented frequencies of about 15% is to be noted. The major sources for these exotic stones were the Hudson Valley Deepkill and Normanskill formations, and the Onondaga chert outcrops northwest of them. The yellow jasper may be from Pennsylvania. The origins of the chalcedonies are not known to me, but Maine is a possible source.

Three of the four features assigned a Stratum 2 provenience (table 7) were pits with pink ash. Features 19, 28, and 41 were recognized and recorded near the base of Stratum 3, but were certainly intrusive to that depth from an occupation floor or floors since obliterated by the plow zone (chapter 2). Feature 19 was dated; Feature 41 had grit-tempered, rocker-stamped sherds in it, and probably a corner-notched point (pls. 19n and 20). Feature 38 was a Colonial period trench observed in N3E2 just below the plow zone; a posthole 8 inches in diameter was 6 inches south of the trench wall. It is just possible that this combination marks an eighteenth-century fence line north of the Stark house. It is older than the plow zone which cut it.

Stratum 2 is not properly an accumulation unit, as are those below it. Obviously, it is an artifact of eighteenth- and nineteenth-century plowing and in one sense had its beginning then. Its terminal date, around 1842, is well established by historical records and internal evidence. In order to understand the relationship of Stratum 2 to the rest of the site, it is necessary to estimate the age of the oldest deposits incorporated into it. Below it, Stratum 3 included *in situ* materials at least 3,600 years old — the Atlantic artifacts. Nothing younger appeared there except in intrusive pits. The Wayland Notched point in Stratum 2, about 3,500 years old (Dincauze 1968, p. 76), is likely to be among the oldest artifacts *in situ* there. All of the ceramic-using occupations, at least, were churned into Stratum 2, and apparently some terminal Archaic deposits were incorporated also. The only direct indication of the age of the prehistoric deposits in Stratum 2 is the age of Feature 19 — 395 ± 90 radiocarbon years.

4

Cultural History and Activities

The locale that is now northern Manchester has been inhabited by people for 10,000 to 11,000 years. In those hundred centuries a lot of trash accumulated; some of the less destructible items were the basis for this study. With the refuse as a guide, we have been able to learn something about the cultural traditions and work habits of those people who left us no other account of themselves. This chapter will summarize the interpretations derived from the analyses of artifact forms and stratigraphic relationships which were reported in chapters 1 through 3. Some data on regional paleoecology will be introduced, to enrich the context of the cultural activity.

EARLIEST OCCUPANTS

Some artifacts recovered at the Neville site are older than the river terrace on which the site was located. They must have been left originally in some other spot, from which they were collected by later people. Being older than the terrace itself, they are necessarily older than the Falls, which formed by continuing erosion after the river had cut the terrace.

These older artifacts include the tip of a fluted point made of jasper, which was found at the interface between Strata 1 and 2. Its age of 10,000-11,000 years is estimated by comparison with the radiocarbon age of the Debert site in Nova Scotia, where similar tools were found in large numbers (MacDonald 1968). Four flake tools from Stratum 5B are closely comparable to others found elsewhere with fluted points, and they are quite distinct, in raw material, form, and manufacturing technique, from anything else in 5B (pls. 7j-l; 8e). There must have been a camp or camps of Paleo-Indian peoples not far from Amoskeag, where the first inhabitants of the Neville site could pick up these attractive old tools. Later styles of spearheads, illustrated on plates 8a

118

and 6d, are like those made farther south about nine and eight thousand years ago, respectively (Coe 1964; Broyles 1971). They must have been brought to the site from older camps also. The only glimpses we have of the earliest occupants of the locale are this selection of pieces dropped by the Neville inhabitants. Those fragments tell us only about hunting, cutting, and scraping activities.

With the Falls not yet formed, the landscape and natural resources of the locale were obviously different from those which shaped human activities later. The river ran at a higher level, in a broader, shallower valley. The river itself may have run shallow, with meanders and braided channels, so that in drier seasons lots of fine sand was available, on exposed bars, for wind transportation. Dunes formed on the east side of the valley. There were probably fish in the streams – perhaps fewer than later and perhaps of a different species composition – in the early years when glaciers and snowfields in the White Mountains kept the water temperatures low. The climate was cooler than it was for the Neville terrace inhabitants; the forests had fewer deciduous trees and more northern conifers (Davis 1969). The fauna, also, must have been of a more northern type, perhaps with woodland caribou as the major herbivore, later replaced by moose and elk.

The living sites of the Paleo-Indians and Early Archaic inhabitants of the locality must have been situated to exploit resources unlike those used later. They will be hard to find, especially as they are probably buried under many feet of windblown sand. Deep excavations for commercial and industrial purposes should be checked carefully; the early sites will be exposed accidentally if at all.

MIDDLE ARCHAIC OCCUPANTS

The climate was warmer by the time the Neville terrace was available for occupancy. In southern New England generally, mixed pine-oak forest was established and was expanding north by 8,500 years ago; it was replaced by an oak-hemlock flora in the south by 6,000 years ago (Davis 1965, p. 388). It is possible, therefore, that the first occupants of the terrace were surrounded by a forest only a little more boreal in composition than that of the eighteenth century A.D. Deer and moose probably had replaced caribou in the expanding Merrimack lowland. The river had reached bedrock at Amoskeag, and was eroding downstream from the sill to form the falls. The river must have been swarming with anadromous fish in late spring. The incipient falls would have slowed them enough locally to make them easy game for the fishermen. Windblown dust had just begun to accumulate on the terrace surface when the first campfires were lighted there to cook or smoke the fish, to whose remains we can trace the concentration of mercury in the soil.

The Neville Complex

The first fishermen brought to Amoskeag a cultural tradition which had developed along the Atlantic seaboard and piedmont to the south of New England (Coe 1964). Arriving at Amoskeag no more than a few centuries after 8000 B.P., they must have been expanding their range as their habitat expanded. In warm seasons, these fishermen may have exceeded the range of the mixed oak forest to which they were well adapted.

The raw materials of the tools they brought with them indicate a downstream origin, or at least trading partners, near the Merrimack estuary. The tool kit they left on the terrace, here labeled the "Neville complex," contains artifacts like those recovered from other sites along the Merrimack and its tributaries. The same types of tools have been found widely throughout Massachusetts, Rhode Island, and Connecticut.

The Neville complex includes: Neville and Neville variant points; perhaps also Stark points; unhafted flake scrapers of steep-bitted, beaked, or casual form; and the tiny quartz crystal crapers. Wedge-shaped unhafted flake knives, like the scrapers, are old, conservative tool forms which were made for a thousand or more years. Perforators were the simple shaft kind or had bases like Neville points, and were used, at least sometimes, for reaming holes. Biface preforms, with rounded or flat bases, were preliminary steps in the production of other tools. Pebble, core, and angular cobble hammers were used for hard work; softer hammers of organic materials were used in stone knapping. Probably only the hard hammers could have produced the quartz crystal polyhedrons. Heavy flaked choppers for rough work and tabular whetstones for making and maintaining other tools complete the inventory.

With these tools, and others of organic substances, the Neville complex people procured and processed their food, made and maintained their shelters and equipment. The scrapers were used primarily on hard materials such as wood or bone. One of them may have sharpened the stake (Feature 22) which showed up so clearly in the subsoil (pl. 2b), and perhaps others like it, which were used to support shelters or fish-drying racks. The scarcity of hide-working wear on scrapers suggests that skins were not cured and softened at this site. Knives were used for cutting and slicing; the substance they shaped is unknown. Pits with charcoal-rich fill may have been hearths; the evidence is incomplete. The association of stone hammers with such pits is not interpreted.

During early visits to the site, the occupants chipped a lot of quartz. Even though hard to work, it was probably the most familiar locally available stone. Eventually, exploring northward, the people became familiar with the volcanic stones of eastern New Hampshire, especially the buff-colored rhyolite from the mountains around Lake Winnipesaukee (appendix). A steady supply of that stone and others in the area freed them from further need to seek supplies downstream, at a much greater distance. A lot of stone knapping was done here; stone tool production may have been a major activity at Amoskeag, with finished tools carried away for use elsewhere.

The soil chemistry is the only direct evidence for fishing at this site. The high concentration of mercury indicates the accumulation of waste matter from the bodies of anadromous fish. The spring fishery at the Falls, during spawning runs, would have been the richest natural resource of the locality, an obvious attraction for spring settlement. The absence of plant-processing tools in the tool kit tends to support the suggestion of a spring camp, since the plant foods available at that season are succulent greens, requiring little preparation for consumption. The evidence against hide-working leads toward the same conclusion; in the spring, animal hides are of poor quality.

The Stark Complex

Living floors on the terrace were successively buried by increments of wind-deposited sand. By the time that Stratum 5A was accumulating, the refuse left by the spring fishermen was slightly different in composition from that sealed below in Stratum 5B. The tool kits of 5A and the lowest levels of 4B are termed the "Stark complex," named for the dominant projectile point style (fig. 9). The duration of the Stark complex can only be estimated. It may have begun before 7000 B.P.; it was superseded some centuries before 6000 B.P.

The assemblage differs in small ways from that of the Neville complex. The Stark style is prominent among the projectile points. Neville and Neville variant points accompany the Starks at first, to be replaced by Merrimacks later. The unhafted scrapers and knives are like those of the Neville complex, except that the quartz crystal scrapers are unimportant and some of the steep flake scrapers have noses on their working edges. Spokeshaves made on flakes appear. Perforators have Stark-style bases or flake bases; the simple shaft style is rare in this context. The large bifacial preforms are present in great quantities. Polyhedral nuclei are no longer made of quartz crystal. Rough flaked choppers continue. Core hammers are present in low numbers; pebble and cobble hammers are absent. Ground stone artifacts are significantly represented by winged atlatl weights and a full-grooved axe, here appearing as early as they are known anywhere else in eastern North America.

The stratigraphic overlap of the three Middle Archaic point styles in these levels of the site raises questions about the coevality or succession of the three styles. The stratigraphic data from this site are insufficiently precise to resolve the question whether the three styles succeeded each other in discrete occupations, with subsequent mixture by pitting, or whether they overlapped significantly in time and were used together by the same peoples. What is clear from the stratigraphy is their relative order in time — the beginnings, peaks, and ends of the three dis-

tribution curves maintain the same order (fig. 9). The analysis of manufacturing technique indicated a technological succession in the same
order: Nevilles and Starks and Starks and Merrimacks share technical
attributes between them; Nevilles and Merrimacks, the stemmed points,
do not share technical attributes. Technologically, but not stylistically,
Starks are intermediate between the other two types. It is barely possible that the Stark points, with their tapered bases, had a special function that complemented the functions of the Neville and Merrimack
stemmed points. If such was the case, there may have been no distinct
Stark complex — only Neville and Merrimack complexes, either of
which could include Starks or not. Association data from isolated com-
ponents at other sites will be needed to resolve the question, but I be-
lieve that a distinct Stark complex, without either Neville or Merrimack
points in it, will be demonstrable.

The basic activities of food procurement and preparation, toolmaking and repairing, continued as before with some innovations of
technology — especially the Stark points themselves. Scrapers were still
used predominantly on hard materials; the spokeshave innovation may
be a special tool for some of the same tasks. The noses on a few scraper
bits are another innovation, the purpose not yet understood. Cutting
and slicing were done with the old unhafted flake knives. Perforators
were made on flakes as well as bifaces, but seem to have been used in
the same ways as before. The artifact ratios (table 9) show that perforators were relatively less common than they had been. Stone knapping
remained an important activity. Buff rhyolite and other New Hampshire volcanic stones, among them some lightly metamorphosed tuffs
and felsites, were the major raw materials. The relative drop in numbers of hammerstones (table 9) may be related to the fact that quartz
was little used at this time (figs. 7 and 8). Roughly flaked choppers
were still employed on occasion. The presence of the full-grooved axe
indicates some serious woodworking. The specimen abandoned here
was still in working condition; it may have been left in expectation of
future use on the site.

The mercury content of the soil testifies to the continuing importance of the spring fishing industry. There is no direct evidence for fishing equipment in the tool kit, unless it is the projectile points themselves. The large salmon could have been speared successfully. Dip nets
would have been more efficient tools for taking shad, alewives, and
lampreys, but there is no indication of their presence.

The high artifact density index for Stratum 5A (table 6) is hard to
interpret. Without more precise control of the stratigraphy, it is impossible to tell whether the density reflects intensity of site use or mechan-
ical enrichment through pitting. The soil chemistry is also equivocal,
with the relatively low phosphorous value in apparent contradiction

with the artifact density. The two can be reconciled only if soil Sample C was drawn from the very top of Stratum 5A, where artifact frequencies were relatively low and sterile lenses occasionally present (fig. 6).

Merrimack Complex

Prior to the publication of the first report on this site (Dincauze 1971), no discrete Merrimack complex was recognized. Instead, Merrimack points were considered part of the Stark complex. Once all the artifact analyses had been completed, it was obvious that more than a new projectile point style distinguished Stratum 4B from those below it. New scraper types appeared; and other inventory changes indicated a distinct assemblage in 4B. The Merrimack complex shares the greater part of its inventory with its two predecessors; there is no doubt about its special relationship with them within a single developing cultural tradition. It is the youngest unit of that tradition at the Neville site, where its last appearance occurred close to 6,000 radiocarbon years ago.

Merrimack points dominate the assemblage, especially above the lowest level of 4B. They are accompanied by Starks throughout the stratum, but the numbers of Stark points decline steadily. The ancient unhafted flake tools continue – the steep-bitted flake scrapers, some with noses, the beaked scrapers, the casual flake scrapers, and the wedge-shaped knives. The polyhedrons reach their peak frequencies; some have tiny scraperlike noses on them. Two new types of scrapers appear, both made on flake-blades, and each showing a distinct use pattern. The carinated scrapers have the rounded, striated bits characteristic of end scrapers used on hides (pl. 23e). Three of the thick end scrapers have ventral use scars, developed as the tool was pushed along a tough surface like a plane. The perforators have only an unspecialized biface base; no Merrimack bases or simple shaft perforators occur. The unfinished axe blank may belong with either the Stark or Merrimack complexes. Winged atlatl weights continued in use, with the best specimen (pl. 14c) associated with this complex. Core hammers and angular cobble hammers occur in relatively low numbers (table 9). Two full-grooved pebbles lay on the uppermost occupation floor (pl. 16e), more than 20 feet apart. There were no choppers.

The features observed on the 4B/A interface included three charcoal concentrations, a pit intruding to Stratum 5A, and a cobble arrangement with charcoal (pl. 2a), which included the largest angular cobble hammer.

The Merrimack complex reflects some differences in the major site activities in comparison with the earlier Stark and Neville complexes. Artifact density drops, but only a little. Anadromous fish were still taken, perhaps in smaller numbers. Toolmaking and repairing activities continued, but different tools were being made and used. Spokeshaves were not used; and the frequency of scrapers used on hard materials declined. Hide scrapers and scraper-planes indicate new kinds of work being done. Knapping remained an important activity, which involved New Hampshire volcanic stones and fewer and fewer exotic ones. The buff rhyolite was still procured from the Winnipesaukee-Ossipee region; a suite of aphanitic volcanic rocks and a peculiar gray porphyry were also favored.

Toward the end of the Stratum 4B accumulation period, at least this part of Amoskeag was receiving less intensive occupational use. Artifact frequencies drop (figs. 9, 12, and 13); the concentrations of organic chemicals in the soil decline (table 5, Sample E).

Summary

The Middle Archaic occupations of the site occurred between 7,740± 280 and 5,910±180 radiocarbon years ago. They seem to have been spring fishing camps, exploiting the spawning runs of anadromous fish at a convenient interception point. The wide variety of tasks performed here and the large numbers of heavy tools deposited imply that this was a base camp, where both industrial and domestic chores were routinely accomplished.

After an initial period of exploration, there is evidence for increasing knowledge of and dependence upon local lithic resources. Familiarity with regional resources of all kinds certainly paralleled knowledge of rocks. By the time of the Merrimack complex, if not well before, the people who fished at Amoskeag probably spent their entire annual cycle in the region. Their abrupt disappearance after 5910 B.P. is perplexing.

The cultural tradition exposed here has significant close relationships with Middle Archaic cultures of the Atlantic seaboard and piedmont far to the south. The stemmed projectile point forms and the flake tools which accompany them are directly related to even older complexes in the Southeast. The ultimate southern derivation of the tradition, and its very ancient roots, are considered to be amply demonstrated. The expansion of this tradition northward took place synchronously with the expansion of mixed oak forests during the postglacial climatic warming.

HIATUS AND REOCCUPATION

The very small numbers of artifacts in the lowest levels of Stratum 4A led the excavators to hypothesize a gap in site occupancy at the time those levels were accumulating . The analyses reported in chapters 2 and 3 support and augment this idea. Middle Archaic tool types virtually disappear above the 4A/B interface (figs. 9, 12, and 13). Actual artifact counts are indeed low. Some of the few items present seem to have been intruded from higher levels, where their types are more common (fig. 10). Those artifacts which appear to be *in situ* in these levels belong to a cultural tradition which derives from the west, in the Great Lakes and Ohio River drainages, rather than from the Atlantic drainage.

The appearance of the new cultural tradition, even more than the paucity of artifacts, is suggestive of a temporary abandonment of the site. Nothing about the handful of projectile points and the few objects associated with them implies the appearance of a vigorous, militant population sufficiently forceful to dislodge a successful resident population. Aggressive, competitive replacement is highly unlikely. The newcomers appear to have trickled in to a temporarily depopulated region.

This replacement is not an isolated incident confined to this one site. A similar set of circumstances has been recognized at a site in the Connecticut Valley in northern Massachusetts. Many possible explanations have been proposed in conversations I have had with other New England researchers, but none has been supported strongly by currently available evidence. This report will not be encumbered further with speculation. It is enough to urge research into climatic, ecological, and cultural factors which might have contributed to the withdrawal of Middle Archaic peoples from some of their favorite fishing stations and to the expansion of interior cultures into southern New England between 5,000 and 6,000 years ago.

Vosburg and Otter Creek Points

The first projectile points dropped onto the vacated campsite appear to be Vosburg and Otter Creek types (pl. 9l, m, n). Brewerton Side-Notched points apparently are equally early. A slate knife was close to all three types in the center of the site. The associations can represent no more than one or more brief visits by a few people, perhaps only hunters. There is no evidence for the season of their visits. One of the Vosburg-like basal fragments is made of a porphyritic stone favored by the Merrimack makers. Local manufacture and repair of equipment is indicated by this observation and by the presence of a few chert chips in these levels.

LATE ARCHAIC OCCUPANTS

The interrupted occupational history at the Neville site alerts us to the possibility that climatic or ecological crises made the area less attractive to human settlement for a while. The Amoskeag locale's position at the northern end of the Merrimack lowland, on the boundary of the New England Upland, makes it particularly sensitive to minor fluctuations of climate, which may be locally intensified by the valley morphology and orientation. In the absence of any direct paleoecological data from the region,·no attempt at reconstruction will be made here.

The low mercury concentration in Stratum 4A may reflect an impoverishment of the fishery resource at Amoskeag. It may, however, have been caused by a shift of activity locus to some other part of the river bank or by an entirely noncultural edaphic factor.

Brewerton Complex(es)

Brewerton Side-Notched points, which were among the earliest post-hiatus artifacts, occur at the next highest excavation level with Brewerton Eared-Notched points, fragments of ground stone tools, a ground slate knife, ocher, graphite, and a paint-grinder. In the same southern area of the site, at the next highest level, Brewerton Eared-Notched and Brewerton Eared-Triangle points were associated. This provides some tentative stratigraphic support for Ritchie's typological seriation of these three styles in eastern New York (Ritchie 1961, pp. 17-20).

None of the Brewerton points are made of materials otherwise represented at the site; they were probably brought in from elsewhere. The use of pigments is an unprecedented activity at the site. Otherwise, not much more than a temporary hunting camp is represented, and there is no evidence for seasonality. A brief visit or visits by small groups of people seem to be represented by the small inventory. However, the clustering at the southern end of the site may be no more than the fringe of a more impressive deposit farther south.

All the Brewerton points lay at or below the level of the 4390±180 B.P. charcoal sample, which is here accepted as an age indicator for upper Stratum 4A. This *terminus ante quem* is only slightly older than the age of the Brewerton deposit at the Hornblower II site on Martha's Vineyard (Ritchie 1969b, p. 220). It does suggest that the Hornblower date is a terminal age referent and that southern New England Brewerton complexes are likely to be closer to 4,500 than 4,200 radiocarbon years old.

Small Point Tradition

Two styles (stemmed and triangular) and several types of small points are present in upper Stratum 4A and Stratum 3. Probably because of the extensive disturbance of those zones by Woodland pits, the stratigraphy is not especially enlightening in respect to the relative order of the several types. Among the stemmed points, those provisionally designated small stemmed II are the earliest (fig. 10). The points which are closest to Ritchie's Wading River type appear to begin somewhat later. Only two points were recognized as Squibnocket Stemmed, and they were in the uppermost levels of Stratum 3. The triangular forms are harder to seriate and even more difficult to type confidently. The Beekman form with the nearly straight base disappears before the last of the

Squibnocket triangles. There are too few small notched triangles to place. The total numbers of projectile points exceed those shown on figure 10, which excludes minor types and untypable pieces.

There is no assemblage at the Neville site which corresponds to the Squibnocket complex of Martha's Vineyard (Ritchie 1969b), although the latest group of projectile points – Squibnocket Triangles, Squibnocket Stemmed points, Wading River points – is similar. The heavy tools of that complex are entirely absent here, as are the flake knives; the scrapers and perforators of Strata 4A and 3 have no parallels in the Vineyard sites. The scrapers associated with the points are, like the latter, predominantly made of quartz. Expanded-bit, biface, and angled scrapers all seem to be made for socket hafts. Biface base and simple shaft perforators complete the chipped stone industry. There is one gouge bit fragment possibly associated, and angular cobble hammers. Graphite may be associated.

Possible cultural differences aside, it is obvious that the activities engaged in at Amoskeag were very different from those undertaken at Vineyard shellheaps. There is some question about the importance of anadromous fish to the small point inhabitants of Amoskeag. The mercury concentration is very low throughout Stratum 4A, and even though it rises in 3, it never achieves earlier values (table 5). The sediment study shows a significantly enlarged B fraction (fig. 5), coarser than the wind-blown dust which comprises most of the deposit. This coarse fraction was composed of river sand and crushed burned bone. Under magnification, none of the bone was obviously piscine; many fragments showed articular surfaces which seem to be from very small mammals. No pestles or mullers were recovered with these crushed bones. Small mammals are likely to be snared or trapped rather than shot. Their role in the total diet cannot be evaluated. Quartz was the preferred lithic raw material, for the first time since the initial occupations of the terrace. The stemmed and triangular points must have been hafted and used differently, but there is no evidence here which helps distinguish their functions. The biface and expanded-bit scrapers were similarly used, on hard materials; they may be functional equivalents, with expanded-bit scrapers replacing the earlier bifacial form. The angled scrapers may have been side scrapers, or a kind of knife. The vertical displacement of many specimens of small points and scrapers (figs. 10 and 12) may record pit digging from these levels, but very few features were recognized. A few hearths were recorded. The activities seem more restricted in scope than would be expected at a base camp. The Neville terrace may have been only a special-activity area for a major settlement elsewhere. Heavy occupation of the bluff top to the east had begun by Late Archaic times; the base camp may have been there.

The stratigraphic relationships are not clear enough to establish whether or not the small point occupation was in fact coeval with any ·of the Brewerton occupations. It is possible that the Brewerton Eared-Notched and Eared-Triangle points overlapped in time with the earliest of the small points, as their stratigraphic overlap indicates (fig. 10).

The age of 4390±180 B.P. for the small point occupation in Stratum 4A is very reasonable. It falls between the ages of similar points at the Hornblower II and Bear Swamp sites in southeastern Massachusetts (Ritchie 1969b, p. 220; Staples and Athearn 1969, p. 5). The bulk of the small point occupations occurs above the radiocarbon sampling locality, in Stratum 3, implying continuity well beyond that time.

In the 1971 report, it was implied that cultural continuity existed between the Merrimack points and the early small stemmed points. The more detailed analysis since completed does not support that opinion. There is no demonstration at this site for development or any close relationship between Merrimack and any small stemmed Late Archaic points. The stratigraphically lowest small stemmed points are very likely intrusive below their respective living floors and do not approach Merrimacks in age.

Atlantic Complex

Near the base of Stratum 3 appear a few artifacts of early Susquehanna tradition affiliations. In formal conception, manufacturing technique, and raw materials they contrast strongly with the small quartz artifacts among which they were found.

The artifacts include an Atlantic spearpoint and knife found in adjacent squares in successive excavation units, ovoid biface scrapers, and a fragment of a winged atlatl weight (pl. 9a, b, e).

The indicated activities are few: hunting and hide preparation. The cluster of ovoid scrapers in the southern part of the excavated area hints at a special activity area there: hide scraping spatially distinct from other tasks. The projectile point and knife were 40 feet farther north.

So little evidence for hide-working was observed among all the artifacts from the site that this group is almost unique. It may represent a brief hunting camp occupation, perhaps in the fall, which was unrelated to the normal seasonal use of the site. The contrast suggests one way in which peoples of different cultural traditions could utilize a single site with minimal conflict. It is regrettable that evidence for the seasonality of small point occupations was inconclusive. In any case, the brief appearance of Atlantic complex artifacts at the site does not seem to mark the end, or even an interruption, of the small point tradition occupations.

Summary

The initial reoccupation of the site, following the hiatus in the sixth millennium B.P., occurred from the west, when Vosburg, Otter Creek, and then Brewerton point users brought cherts and other exotic stones to Amoskeag.

From then on, the range of activities pursued at the site seems to have been narrower than it was during the Middle Archaic occupations. There are fewer artifacts and fewer functional classes of artifacts. The main focus of occupation may have shifted from the terrace to other parts of the locale.

Following the Brewerton complex, possibly overlapping with the last part of it, the small point tradition was the dominant cultural manifestation. Despite the strong morphological similarity between some of the small stemmed points and Merrimacks, there is no evidence here for any derivation of the former from the latter. The artifacts which accompany the projectile points in each case are totally distinct, with the possible exception of angular cobble hammers. This is the more surprising as the small point tradition seems to be indigenous to the Atlantic watershed and to have relatives far to the south, as was true of the Middle Archaic complexes.

The Atlantic complex made a brief appearance, announcing the arrival of the Susquehanna tradition in the region. Other Later Archaic cultural complexes are represented minimally in the collection. Two narrow, long-stemmed points resemble forms which are most common on the central coast of Maine (pl. 9c, d), and a single chert Normanskill point must be a Hudson Valley souvenir (pl. 9k).

The dearth of ground stone tools in these Late Archaic assemblages presents a significant contrast to conditions at many other southern New England sites. It is worth mentioning that no axes, plummets, pestles, or mullers, and very few adzes, atlatl weights, and hammerstones are in evidence in the Late Archaic occupation levels.

LATER OCCUPANTS

The cultural history of the last 3,500 years is either all compressed and commingled in Strata 2 and 1 or scattered in pits and trenches throughout the site. The prehistory cannot be known in any detail. Fortunately, the prehistoric sequence for this time period in southern New England is known in outline. The many styles of projectile points, at least, have been typed and dated, or can be compared to types with known temporal ranges. The pottery can be distinguished, at least, as early or late. Very few other objects in the old plow zone remain to be accounted for. What follows is simply a brief summary of the several complexes whose presence can be inferred.

Susquehanna Tradition Complexes

A scatter of projectile points and a perforator can be related to two or three post-Atlantic complexes of the Susquehanna tradition, which belong to the time period between 3600 and 2700 B.P. (Dincauze 1968). The earlier years of this span saw the appearance of a Susquehanna Broad point of Onondaga chert, Wayland Notched points of the Dudley and Coburn varieties, and a perforator with a Wayland base (pls. 9f; 13j). Sometime within the later four or five centuries, an Orient point was dropped (pl. 9g). Probably the Susquehanna presence was minimal here; otherwise, many typical Susquehanna scrapers, knives, heavy tools, and steatite sherds were plucked from the plow zone over a century ago. Two otherwise unexplained radiocarbon ages (table 8, Samples 2529 and 1920) might be referable to Susquehanna activities, if the charcoal samples were in fact in unobserved pits some two feet deep.

Woodland Complexes

Paleoclimatological data from many sources converge to indicate a change from warm to cooler climates about 3,000 years ago. Atmospheric radiocarbon activity increased, which has been observed to occur during cooler climatic episodes (Denton and Karlén 1973, Fig. 1). Deep-sea sediment studies in the Atlantic indicate that ". . . there was a major shift from warm to colder climate about 3,000 years ago. . ." marking the end of the postglacial warm period which began about 7,800 years ago (Wollin, Ericson, and Ewing 1971). Alpine glaciers advanced in western North America and in Scandinavia (Denton and Karlén 1973, Fig. 1). In southern New England, the forest composition had changed from oak-hickory to oak-chestnut by 2000 B.P. (Davis 1965, p. 389).

The only observation at Neville which may reflect this change is the probability of a slower rate of sedimentation above Stratum 3. The nine inches incorporated into Stratum 2 apparently represent over 3,000 years of accumulation, while the four feet of sediment below it aggraded in about five thousand years. These comparative figures are only suggestive, since we have no information at all about the cultural processes which may have affected accumulation and erosion during the last 3,000 years of prehistory at the site.

The change from Archaic to Woodland adaptive patterns elsewhere in New England appears to be related to the climatic change in its many manifestations (Dincauze 1974). We can only assume that the use of the site during the Woodland occupations reflected the new conditions.

Early and Middle Woodland

The sequence of ceramic-using Woodland cultures of the last 3,000 years begins with the Meadowood phase (Ritchie 1969a, pp. 180-200).

Meadowood points, bifacial trianguloid scrapers, and perforators, mostly of New York cherts, appear in the collection (pls. 12j; 13o, p). Similar, unnamed side-notched points are likely to be of the same age (pl. 12k, l). A few untyped stemmed points may relate to the Early Woodland Lagoon type of south coastal New England (pl. 12f, g, h; Ritchie 1969b, p.245). Rossville points of Early to Middle Woodland affiliations are represented by only three specimens (pl. 12m). Early ceramics include sherds of Vinette I type (pl. 19a) and others of similar coarse wares with corded surfaces.

Middle Woodland Ceramic styles are illustrated on plate 19d, l, n, o and on plates 20 and 21. Some may be coeval with Rossville points, others belong with lanceolate bifaces like those shown on plate 12c, d, e. The corner-notched point shown on plate 20 is believed to have been in Feature 41 with the rocker-stamped sherds.

Late Woodland

Levanna points, pressure-flaked from fine-grained silicates, and Levanna-like points, percussion flaked from felsites, are the hallmarks of the Late Woodland period of southern New England. They were the dominant stone point type from about A.D. 900 until they were replaced by European metal and guns. Late Woodland ceramics are not well dated or seriated anywhere in New England. Comparison with style sequences in New York State and some regional evidence (Dincauze 1975) suggest that sherds decorated with cord-wrapped stick impressions or with incised hachures and parallel lines are of Late Woodland age. Collared vessels and all sherds of fine-textured thin wares were considered to be Late Woodland. Representative examples are illustrated on plate 19b, c, e-k, m. All the collars in this collection are narrow. There are many instances of notched lips on vessels with Late Woodland or very late Middle Woodland attributes. The notched lips and narrow collars may have regional significance. Only one ceramic type defined elsewhere (eastern New York) was recognized among these sherds; a probable Chance Incised rimsherd is shown on plate 19k.

Three English pipes and a glass bead mark the end of the Late Woodland period and the beginning of historic time at Amoskeag.

General Woodland

A very few scrapers, notably the long-flake end scrapers (pl. 13m), can be related to Woodland occupations without greater specificity. The semicircular slate pendant is similarly attributed (pl. 14d). No other artifacts survive to inform about activities here during the thirty Woodland centuries.

The peculiar pink ash lenses in some of the Woodland pits are unexplained. Equally puzzling is the nonrandom distribution of pits with potsherds which were strongly clustered along and west of the major north-south trench. There are no pit counts from which to quantify this observation; it was made on the basis of plots of potsherds recovered below Stratum 2.

The great variety of lithic materials in Stratum 2 presents an interesting contrast to the situation in strata below. The dominance of quartz in Strata 3 and upper 4A suggested fairly local procurement of raw materials during the occupations of the Late Archaic small point tradition. The New Hampshire rhyolite which dominated Strata 4B and 5A suggested standardized regional procurement patterns for the Middle Archaic. However, in Stratum 2, there was a bewildering diversity of lithics, including silicates from New York, Pennsylvania, and possibly Maine (chalcedonies and agates). Local and regional rocks are not in the majority. At the very least, this situation indicates a more cosmopolitan communications network involving Amoskeag during the last three millennia, contrasting with the parochialism of part of the Late Archaic and the regional self-sufficiency of the Middle Archaic periods.

5

Summary and Conclusions

The results of this study of the Neville site have significance for the prehistory of (1) the immediate locale, (2) the southern New England region, and (3) the Atlantic coastal area. Within all those spatial frames, the site has relevance for cultural sequence and chronology, adaptive patterns, culture history, and methodology.

THE AMOSKEAG LOCALE

At the level of site and locale, all the conclusions presented above have relevance. Only the major contributions will be summarized here. The first occupation of the site, which occurred over 7,700 radiocarbon years ago, followed earlier habitation in the neighborhood. From that time until 6,000 years ago, the people using the site shared a single developing cultural tradition which originated to the south of New England along the Piedmont and Coastal Plain physiographic provinces. The people were attracted to the site by the seasonal abundance of anadromous fish, which could be taken at Amoskeag Falls. They made a base camp near the fishing spot and carried on a wide range of activities. The activities were organized to maintain life while exploiting local and regional resources such as the fish, other early summer edible foods, and ancient volcanic rocks which were obtained farther upstream. The exploitation of regional resources increased in diversity, and probably intensity, through time. The cultural changes dimly perceived in the sequence were partly adaptive responses based on increasing familiarity with the local resources.

The site was essentially abandoned for an unknown period of time between 6000 and 5000 B.P. Reoccupation began before the latter date, with brief visits by peoples whose cultural affiliations were to the west and north. The cultural sequence for the last 5,000 years appears to have been normal for southern New England. In contrast to the single cultural tradition during the 2,000 years of the Middle Archaic period, there were at least three traditions represented in the Late

Archaic period, between 6,000 and 3,000 years ago. Specific evidence for resource exploitation and seasonality of site use is scarce for the latter period; the data suggest that the site was a special-purpose area during that time, not a base camp as it had been previously.

The last 3,500 years of occupancy is all jumbled in the lower plow zone, further restricting the information content of the remains. Apparently, the range of activities carried on at the site continued to narrow. Increasing diversity of lithic raw materials, and some few western styles of ceramic vessels, imply greater complexity in the communication networks in which Amoskeag residents participated. Both trends imply increasing specialization of tasks and of resource exploitation through time, which probably reflects growing population density and the social and economic interdependence which normally accompanies it.

However, interpretations about adaptive patterns at this scale of generalization cannot be supported with data only from one site. The evidence from the Smyth site nearby is essential to test and elaborate the outline of adaptive strategies proposed for the Neville site, especially since intensive use of the Smyth site appears to have begun only in the Late Archaic period.

THE SOUTHERN NEW ENGLAND REGION

In spite of its marginal position in southeastern New Hampshire, in terms of its culture history the Merrimack lowland is part of southern New England. The sequence of cultural units through the last 5,000 years is very close to that reported on Martha's Vineyard. Similarly, the main elements of the Middle Archaic sequence have regional implications.

Recognition of the age and significance of the Middle Archaic assemblages in southern New England was long delayed. The initial demonstration of Middle Archaic artifact styles stratified below those of the Late Archaic was made by Ripley P. Bullen in 1946, when he reported stemmed points below small quartz triangles at several sites in the lower Merrimack drainage in Massachusetts (Bullen 1946a, 1946b). However, compressed stratigraphy and inadequate typological distinctions led to confusion about the meaning of the observed relationship, and its significance remained obscure until 1968 (Dincauze 1972, p. 43). In a series of commentaries and essays between 1952 and 1968, William S. Fowler championed the concept of an "Early Archaic" culture which was identified by projectile points essentially equivalent to the Neville and Stark types here defined, among others (Fowler 1952, 1954, 1968a, 1968b, and others). Neither Fowler nor any of his informants published the detailed data necessary to substantiate their claims of great antiquity for the artifacts, and the unverified and uninterpreted conclusions were accepted by few.

The Neville sequence embodies what may be an important clue to the elusiveness of stratigraphic demonstrations of the Middle Archaic presence in New England. The cultural unconformity after 6000 B.P. divides the Middle Archaic complexes from all later manifestations at the site. With reoccupation, the site is seen to have played a somewhat different role in the local settlement systems than it had before. This change in site-use patterning probably accounts for the relative rarity of Late Archaic occupations stratified over earlier ones. Site locational criteria shifted between the Middle and Late Archaic periods (cf. Dincauze 1974).

Sequence

The overriding significance of the Neville site excavations was the conclusive demonstration of Archaic cultures in the eighth millennium B.P. in southern New England. In addition, the multiple correspondences between the Neville and Doerschuk site cultural sequences aided understanding of the source and origins of these early occupations. Their presence as far north as Amoskeag obviously implies their prior and coeval existence elsewhere in southern New England.

The continuity between the Stark and Merrimack complexes at the Neville site may have more limited relevance than the Neville-Stark sequence which preceded it. Merrimack points are present, but not numerous, downstream in the Merrimack basin (Bullen 1949, Plate III nos. 12, 25). To date, they have not been recognized farther south than the Greater Boston area.

With the Merrimack complex at least a local, if not regional development from the Stark complex, the continuity of a single cultural tradition for 2,000 years is demonstrated. Middle Archaic cultures were firmly established in southern New England until at least 6000 B.P.

The occupational hiatus at 6000 B.P. presents the prehistorian with major regional problems. The disappearance of the Middle Archaic occupants and the subsequent appearance of inland cultural manifestations remain unexplained. What is clear is that there are no local antecedents for the Vosburg-Otter Creek-Brewerton complexes in the Middle Archaic period. Nowhere in New England is a site recognized where the transition from Middle Archaic to Late Archaic cultures can be observed.

The dominance of the small point tradition during the Late Archaic period seems clearer at this site than at most others known. Beginning about 4,500 years ago, perhaps coevally with the latest Brewerton occupations, the small point tradition continued without interruption past the time of the Atlantic complex appearance at the site — about a thousand years. How much later it may have lasted cannot be learned at Neville, because of the plow zone of Stratum 2.

The idea of regional coexistence of the small point tradition and at least the early manifestations of the Susquehanna tradition is supported here (Ritchie 1969b, p. 219). It needs to be carefully tested at sites where activity patterns of both traditions can be observed in detail. Such data are needed to understand the mechanisms of coexistence in this interesting case. It is of considerable theoretical interest to know whether the societies represented by these two distinct traditions related to each other by conflict or complementarity.

Seasonality and Settlement Systems

The excavation strategy adopted at Neville — 3-inch arbitrary excavation units in discrete 5-foot squares — was dictated by limitations of time. It is not an ideal, or even a recommended, strategy for learning about site-specific activities. Therefore, it was interesting and gratifying to see how much activity data could be wrung from the artifact analyses alone. Wear-pattern studies and assemblage comparisons have provided useful first approximations to activity-pattern data. The Neville tool kits and complexes should take on new significance when adequate details are available from other sites where contrasts can be defined.

The Middle Archaic complexes provide the best data on seasonality and activities. The evidence summarized in chapter 4 led to the conclusion that the site was a late spring-early summer base camp during the Middle Archaic period. A wide range of subsistence, maintenance, and manufacturing activities was carried on there, sustained by the fish spawning runs. The tool complexes recognized there are not repeated at all sites where Middle Archaic assemblages have been recovered. The small bog-margin and stream-bank sites found in the Shawsheen and Cochato river valleys of eastern Massachusetts contained rather different complexes of tools (Bullen 1949; Ayres et al. 1955; Cote 1958). Detailed comparisons cannot be made from the literature because of biases in sampling and reporting. However, differences emerge. Semilunar ground stone knives, bifacial chipped knives, plummets, and gouges have been reported in association with Stark and Neville points at several small freshwater sites in eastern Massachusetts (Bullen 1949, pp. 30-31; Ayres et al. 1955; Engstrom 1951, p. 7; Carlson 1964, p. 32). The absence of all these artifacts (with the possible exception of the gouge) from the complexes at the Neville site is suggestive of seasonal differences in tool kits and, presumably, activities. Most of the small site associations remain to be demonstrated conclusively.

The importance of ground stone tools in the Middle Archaic of the Northeast has only recently been recognized. Some early examples of

stone grinding have been briefly summarized by Ritchie (1971a, p. 2).
The atlatl weights and full-grooved axes at the Neville site are close to
7,000 years old. Semilunar ulus and gouges may be equally ancient.
This conclusion requires some adjustment of habitual attributions of
such ground stone tools, which can no longer be considered horizon
styles of the Late Archaic period. Possible complementarity in the distributions of ground stone tools must be considered. For example, the
axes at Neville and the gouges and ulus at the smaller sites may be clues
to seasonality of occupation. We need to sharpen our interpretations of
such associations.

The contrast between the Squibnocket complex of Martha's Vineyard shellheaps and the small point complex(es) at Neville has been
mentioned already in chapter 4. Again, task-specific tool kits must account for some of the differences, since there is so little correspondence
of functional classes. The Atlantic complex at Neville, with its hide-
working scrapers, is suggestive of a special short-term use of the site for
work not usually done there by peoples of other cultural traditions.

The need for elaborated detail on site-specific and seasonal-specific
activities in all periods of Northeastern prehistory is obvious. Research
programs should be planned to meet that need — by selecting sites
where such data can be gathered and by adopting appropriate wide-ex-
posure excavation techniques. Simple stratigraphic excavations for sequence data are no longer high priority needs in southern New England
and can scarcely be justified any more.

Culture History

Three interrelated problems in culture history emerge from the cultural
unconformity between 6000 and 5000 B.P. Why was the site abandoned by the Merrimack people? What brought cultures of western
derivation into central and southern New England? Where and how did
the small point tradition originate, if it cannot be derived from Merrimack directly?

The abandonment could have either a cultural or environmental
cause, or both. The subsequent appearance at the site of interior-adapted
cultures is suggestive of the kind of boundary shift which might be expected as an adaptation to a cooler climate. Direct data on paleoclimates
in central New England are needed to resolve this. Palynology probably
will not provide definitive data on short-term climatic fluctuations of
this scale. The period in question is usually considered to be the height
of the postglacial thermal maximum.

The third question is intimately related to the first two, because a
Middle Archaic cultural complex rather like Merrimack is an attractive
potential ancestor for the Late Archaic small point tradition. Where did
the small point tradition develop? Ritchie has suggested the Middle

Atlantic region (Ritchie 1969b, p. 219). To date, there is little evidence for or against that hypothesis. Extreme southern New England and Long Island, which had larger land areas in those times of lower sea levels, are also possible homelands for the small point tradition. The importance of the quartz pebble industry in that tradition is suggestive of an origin in the glaciated Northeast (Ritchie 1971a, p. 7). A suite of radiocarbon dates from carefully selected contexts could help with this problem as much as a stratified site and might be easier to get. The development sought occurred between 5,500 and 4,600 radiocarbon years ago. There are very few dates from that time period along the Mid-Atlantic coast; Brennan's dates from southern New York suggest that might be a crucial area (Brennan 1972).

Adaptation

For any given region, the course of cultural adaptation can be known only by the compilation of data from a number of different sites. However, at Neville some very general, unidirectional adaptive trends seem to be indicated by changes in the site's role within multisite settlement systems.

Throughout the Middle Archaic period, the site was a seasonal base camp for a community of people. Its location was determined by proximity to the falls, but it was a general-purpose site where a full range of seasonally appropriate activities took place. The community apparently was self-sufficient, utilizing for its needs the resources of a region which extended from Amoskeag to the central New Hampshire lake country.

In the Late Archaic period, the site had become a location where a restricted range of activities took place. It may have been used only by task groups working away from a base camp or by communities staying for very short visits. The implication is that the site was part of more complex settlement systems than had existed previously, in which the annual round of activities took place at a greater number of more specialized locations. The complexity of cultural specialization is reflected also in the existence of three discrete traditions within the period.

The trends toward task diversification and complexity of economic organization seem to continue into the Woodland period. The very small range of functional categories of tools suggests a high degree of task specificity at the site. Even the spatial clustering of pits on the western half of the terrace may be interpreted that way. The number of cultural traditions interacting at various times within the Woodland period has not yet been determined, but it seems that there were at least as many as in the Late Archaic period, and they may have been more restricted in their spatial distributions. Intensification of communication networks and of economic and social interdependence is represented by the high diversity of exotic raw materials and the wide dispersion of design techniques and motifs, both indicating that Amoskeag communities were in contact with peoples as far away as central coastal Maine, the Hudson and Mohawk valleys, and southeastern Massachusetts.

The site thus changed from being a general-purpose location to a special purpose one, even though its main attraction, the fish runs, may have remained the same. The change parallels the adaptive sequence inferred for the Modoc Rock Shelter in southern Illinois on the Prairie/Deciduous Forest boundary. There, Fowler defined a sequence of Archaic adaptive patterns in which adaptation to all the resources of a locale ("Local Adaptation") was followed after 6000 B.P. by "Specialized Adaptation" which involved a proliferation of special-activity sites. The Modoc shelter was a base camp between 8000 and 6000 B.P., a hunting camp afterward (M. Fowler 1959). These changes in site roles presumably reflect changing regional settlement patterns, beginning with seasonal wandering and subsequently developing to central-based wandering.

The development involves increasing specialization of task locations, increasing complexity of communications networks, and increasing interdependence and diversification of social units. These trends are characteristic of increasing sedentariness and rising population density. The close parallels and coincidence of timing between ecological zones as different as southern Illinois and southern New Hampshire indicate the need for more research into the processes involved. Are the determinative factors mainly cultural, relating to critical population densities or to the development of specific, efficient adaptive strategies? Or, is the adaptive change related to some major environmental event, perhaps the stabilization of the northern boundary of the deciduous forest after the postglacial expansion?

THE ATLANTIC COASTAL AREA

Because of the many similarities between the lower levels at Neville and at the Doerschuk site in North Carolina, the Neville sequence has implications for the East Coast area far to the south of it. Brief discussions of these implications have already appeared in print (Dincauze 1971; Ritchie and Funk 1971; Fitzhugh 1972).

The Middle Archaic Period

The Doerschuk Middle Archaic sequence of Stanly and Morrow Mountain complexes was repeated at the Neville site with remarkable fidelity, considering the distances involved. There can be no denying the relatively direct derivation of the northern cultural expression from the southern one, since antecedents are well documented in the south. Such direct derivation must, obviously, involve the territory between, specifically the Middle Atlantic coastal area where an equivalent sequence has yet to be firmly demonstrated.

Stanly points are beginning to be recognized in the Middle Atlantic area, although stratigraphic or radiocarbon demonstration of their age remains to be accomplished there (Ritchie and Funk 1971). The typological similarities between Stark points and Poplar Island points (Kinsey in Ritchie 1961, p. 44) are too close to be fortuitous. The purported Late Archaic age of Poplar Island points is unlikely to be confirmed (pace Kinsey 1971). In fact, there is some evidence already available to indicate that they have considerable antiquity. At Duncan's Island in the lower Susquehanna River, they were found stratified below Late Archaic artifacts, including unspecified Laurentian types (Witthoft 1955) which usually appear at the beginning of the Late Archaic period. It is certain, given the data from Doerschuk and Neville, that Middle Atlantic coast complexes related to Stanly/Neville and Morrow Mountain/Stark will be found and dated to the eighth millennium B.P.

It will be of great interest to know what seventh millennium complexes in the Middle Atlantic region look like. In the Uwharrie sequence, the Guilford complex succeeds Morrow Mountain. At Neville, the Merrimack complex succeeds Stark. These different, apparently coeval, complexes indicate that regional cultural patterns were emerging in the seventh millennium to subdivide the previously unified coastal cultural area. In the Middle Atlantic region, it is possible that a discrete complex with Merrimack-like Bare Island points will be found and dated to the late seventh millennium B.P. If so, continuity between Middle Archaic cultures and the Piedmont tradition with its narrow-stemmed points may be demonstrable, and the historical relationships of the Piedmont-Taconic small point tradition or traditions can be clarified.

The Atlantic Slope Macrotradition

As the foregoing discussion indicates, the entire Atlantic coastal area from North Carolina to New Hampshire was a single cultural province in the eighth millennium B.P. In fact, the province was more extensive, since Stanly or Stanly-like points occur south to Florida, and Neville points are beginning to be recognized in central Maine (Sanger and MacKay 1973, p. 26). Throughout the area east of the Appalachian Mountains, along the Piedmont and Coastal Plain and northeast into the Canadian Maritimes, Middle and Late Archaic cultures as late as the fourth millennium B.P. were characterized by a complex series of stemmed projectile points. It is becoming obvious that the widespread similarities in point styles of various Archaic periods are actually horizon styles and that the Atlantic coast forms a single great culture area with impressive time depth (Fitzhugh 1972).

The area involved is essentially the Atlantic watershed, from eastern

Florida to eastern Canada, exclusive of the Great Lakes and upper St. Lawrence drainage. In 1971, I tentatively introduced the term "Atlantic Slope Archaic" to refer to the ancient stemmed point cultural tradition which was indigenous to this area. Although there has been no stampede to adopt this term, even authors who object to the burden of more terminology find some version of it useful for reference (see Fitzhugh 1972, Figure 2B, "Atlantic Stemmed" culture).

The concept is useful as a high-level abstraction expressing the distinctiveness of East Coast cultures in contrast to the Archaic cultures of the Mississippi drainage, which are characterized by projectile points with notched bases (the Midcontinent tradition of Lewis and Kneberg 1959). The two culture areas impinge upon each other at both the southern and northern ends of the Appalachian divide and are most clearly separated where the mountain watershed is least passable, along the Blue Ridge south of the Potomac. North of the Potomac, the boundaries are much less distinct and shift east and west through time.

The significance of the Blue Ridge divide can be appreciated by comparing the cultural history of the Carolina Piedmont and Coast with that farther north, where trans-Appalachian communication was possible along the Potomac-Cheat gap and through the Susquehanna and Allegheny drainages. In the Carolinas, where isolation from the Midcontinent tradition was greatest, the cultural development from Middle to Late Archaic was apparently conservative. Coe remarked in 1964 upon similarities between the Stanly complex of the Middle Archaic and the Savannah River complex of the Late Archaic, suggesting a fairly direct relationship between them (Coe 1964, pp. 55, 123). This still seems likely, in spite of the appearance of other, distinctive, complexes in intervening times. The Savannah River culture was the ultimate source of the Susquehanna/Broadspear tradition of the Late Archaic, which dominated the Middle Atlantic region in the fourth millennium B.P. and spread north into New England and beyond.

In the Middle Atlantic and New England regions, where contact with the Midcontinent tradition was easier, the development from Middle to Late Archaic cultures followed a somewhat different course. In the Middle Atlantic region, the Piedmont Archaic tradition of narrow-bladed stemmed points developed during the sixth and fifth millennia from undefined Middle Archaic ancestors. During that time, culture contact with the notched point traditions brought Vosburg and Otter Creek-like points eastward toward the coast, where they are scantily represented (Kinsey 1971, pp. 2, 7; 1972, p. 340).

In New England, the presence of Vosburg, Otter Creek, and Brewerton complexes of the sixth and fifth millennia appears to interrupt the development of the Atlantic Slope macrotradition. This interruption is most significant toward the west and north and least clearly demonstrated in the south and southeast. Western Massachusetts, Vermont, New Hampshire, and Maine apparently cannot have been homelands for the nascent small point tradition, but the southern and southeastern coastal areas could have been. Late Archaic cultures of northern New England and eastern Canada are likely to have been derived ultimately (although probably not entirely) from Middle Archaic complexes of the Atlantic Slope macrotradition and thus may be distantly related to the small point tradition farther south.

The concept of the Atlantic Slope macrotradition unites the narrow point traditions of the Northeast (Piedmont, Taconic, and small point) with the Savannah River-Susquehanna broad point traditions through their common ancestry in the Middle Archaic stemmed point complexes. The evidence for this proposed unity is still incomplete; the concept may have to be modified or even abandoned as more is learned about cultures of the sixth and fifth millennia. At the moment, it has some merit and utility, if only to stimulate the research which will ultimately support or refute it.

Appendix

LITHIC MATERIALS

A few general statements on two categories of lithic materials are appended here to stimulate future research in problems of raw materials origins. Collections of specimens from outcrops of the Moat Volcanics of east-central New Hampshire could lead to useful statements about raw materials procurement and communications networks in many periods of prehistory in central New England.

Rhyolite

The buff- to pink-colored phaneric rhyolite which was used so heavily in the Middle Archaic period at the Neville site was not available in the Amoskeag locale. Residues at the site indicate that it was imported in the form of naturally split and weathered talus blocks which were obtained near bedrock outcrops; it was not derived from glacial drift or river gravels.

While visiting the site in 1970, Lincoln Page of the U.S. Geological Survey remarked that the chips closely resembled rhyolites from the Ossipee Mountains near his home in Melvin Village, New Hampshire. Specimens from Ossipee have not been directly compared with the Neville debris; the comparison must be made before the identification can be considered demonstrated.

Among New Hampshire rocks of volcanic origin, only the Moat Volcanics of the east-central part of the state are younger than the regional metamorphism and thus not affected by it (Billings 1956, p. 36). Billings mentions "flesh-colored, or pink porphyritic rhyolites of the Moat Volcanic series on Copple Crown Mountain, southeast of Ossipee,' (ibid., p. 79) but did not map pink or buff rhyolites at Ossipee Mountain. Mr. Page reports (personal communication 4/26/74) that such rock occurs on the south side of the Ossipee Mountains in the vicinity of Bald Knob, in outcrops too small for the scale of Billings's map. Little of the rhyolite at Neville is porphyritic, and none has phenocrysts so large as those described at Copple Crown.

Whether from Ossipee, Copple Crown, or both, the rhyolite at the Neville site apparently came from outcrops of the Moat Volcanics in the vicinity of Lake Winnipesaukee and was brought to Amoskeag by people who selected it for its flaking qualities.

Argillite

This term has been loosely applied here to include a group of lightly metamorphosed fine-grained rocks of sedimentary origin, which occur throughout the sequence at Neville and are probably fairly local in origin. They seem to be fine siltstones, mostly tuffaceous, which are slightly foliated or banded but not slaty. They range in color from black through gray to green and weather mostly to shades of grayish green. When fresh they apparently had reasonably good conchoidal fracture, with some tendency to foliation which produced step fracture. In the soil, some weather deeply, so that the surface is powdery and cannot be handled without damage. Their sources have not been determined, except that they are related to one or another of the volcanic series of eastern New Hampshire.

References

AYRES, K.M., J. BARNES, R. BARNES, W. COTE, G. MELLGREN, D. PRINCE,
E. RUNGE, AND J. WILDER
    1955   "The Indians of the Cochato Valley," *Bulletin of the Massachusetts Archaeological Society*, vol. 16, pp. 48-52.

BAILEY, R.M.
    1938   "The Fishes of the Merrimack Watershed," *Biological Survey of the Merrimack Watershed*. Survey Report #3, pp. 149-185. N.H. Fish and Game Department.

BILLINGS, M.P.
    1956   *The Geology of New Hampshire. Part II – Bedrock Geology.* N.H. State Planning and Development Commission (reprinted 1962).

BRENNAN, L.A.
    1972   "A Vosburg Floor at Montrose Point," *Eastern States Archaeological Federation Bulletin*, no. 31, p. 9.

BROYLES, B.J.
    1971   "Second Preliminary Report: The St. Albans Site, Kanawha County, West Virginia," *Report of Archaeological Investigations No. 3*. West Virginia Geological and Economic Survey.

BULLEN, R.P.
    1946a   "The Foster's Cove Site," *Bulletin of the Massachusetts Archaeological Society*, vol. 7, pp. 24-36.
    1946b   "Suggestions of Stratigraphy in Eastern Massachusetts," *Bulletin of the Massachusetts Archaeological Society*, vol. 7, pp. 54-59.
    1949   *Excavations in Northeastern Massachusetts.* Papers of the R.S. Peabody Foundation for Archaeology, vol. 1, no. 3.

CARLSON, R.W.
    1964   "The Washakumaug Site," *Bulletin of the Massachusetts Archaeological Society*, vol. 25, pp. 29-35.

COE, J.L.

 1964   "The Formative Cultures of the Carolina Piedmont," *Transactions of the American Philosophical Society*, vol. 54, part 5 (reprinted 1971).

COOK, S.F., AND R.F. HEIZER

 1965   *Studies on the Chemical Analysis of Archaeological Sites.* University of California Publications in Anthropology, vol. 2, Berkeley.

COTE, W.

 1958   "Observations and Conclusions Regarding the Archaeology of the Cochato River Valley Area," *Bulletin of the Massachusetts Archaeological Society,* vol. 19, pp. 22-26.

COTTER, J.L.

 1968   *Handbook for Historical Archaeology: Part I.* Wyncote.

DAVIS, M.B.

 1965   "Phytogeography and Palynology of Northeastern United States," in *The Quaternary of the United States,* H.E. Wright, Jr. and D.G. Frey, editors, pp. 377-401, Princeton University Press.

 1969   "Palynology and Environmental History During the Quaternary Period," *American Scientist,* vol. 57, pp. 317-332.

DENTON, G.N., AND W. KARLÉN

 1973   "Holocene Climatic Variations — Their Pattern and Possible Cause," *Journal of Quaternary Research,* vol. 3, pp. 155-205.

DINCAUZE, D.F.

 1968   *Cremation Cemeteries in Eastern Massachusetts.* Papers of the Peabody Museum of Archaeology and Ethnology, Harvard University, vol. 59, no. 1.

 1971   "An Archaic Sequence for Southern New England," *American Antiquity,* vol. 36, pp. 194-198.

 1972   "The Atlantic Phase: A Late Archaic Culture in Massachusetts," *Man in the Northeast,* no. 4, pp. 40-61.

 1973   "Prehistoric Occupation of the Charles River Estuary: A Paleogeographic Study," *Bulletin of the Archaeological Society of Connecticut,* no. 38, pp. 25-39.

 1974   "An Introduction to Archaeology in the Greater Boston Area," *Archaeology of Eastern North America,* vol. 2, no. 1, pp. 39-67, Eastern States Archaeological Federation.

 1975   "Ceramic Sherds from the Charles River Valley," *Bulletin of the Archaeological Society of Connecticut,* no. 39 (in press).

DRAGOO, D.W.

 1973   "Wells Creek — An Early Man Site in Stewart County, Tennessee,' *Archaeology of Eastern North America,* vol. 1, no. 1, pp. 1-55. Eastern States Archaeological Federation.

ENGSTROM, R.E.

1951 "A Preliminary Report on the Nunkatusset Site," *Bulletin of the Massachusetts Archaeological Society*, vol. 13, pp. 5-9.

FENNEMAN, N.M.

1938 *Physiography of Eastern United States*. McGraw-Hill, New York.

FITZHUGH, W.

1972 "The Eastern Archaic: Commentary and Northern Perspective," *Pennsylvania Archaeologist*, vol. 42, pp. 1-19.

FOWLER, M.L.

1959 "Summary Report of Modoc Rock Shelter: 1952, 1953, 1955, 1956," *Report of Investigations No. 8*. Illinois State Museum.

FOWLER, W.S.

1952 "Twin Rivers: Four Culture Sequence at a Rhode Island Site," *Bulletin of the Massachusetts Archaeological Society*, vol. 14, pp. 1-18.

1954 "Rhode Island Prehistory at the Green Point Site," *Bulletin of the Massachusetts Archaeological Society*, vol. 15, pp. 65-80.

1963 "Classification of Stone Implements of the Northeast," *Bulletin of the Massachusetts Archaeological Society*, vol. 25, pp. 1-29.

1968a "Archaic Discoveries at Flat River," *Bulletin of the Massachusetts Archaeological Society*, vol. 29, pp. 17-36.

1968b "A Case for an Early Archaic in New England," *Bulletin of the Massachusetts Archaeological Society*, vol. 29, pp. 53-58.

FUNK, R.E.

1965 "The Archaic of the Hudson Valley — New Evidence and New Interpretations," *Pennsylvania Archaeologist*, vol. 35, pp. 139-160.

FUNK, R.E., AND H. HOAGLAND

1972 "An Archaic Camp Site in the Upper Susquehanna Drainage," *The Bulletin of the New York State Archaeological Association*, no. 56, pp. 11-22.

GARRELS, R.M.

1951 *A Textbook of Geology*. Harper & Bros., New York.

GOLDTHWAIT, J.W., L. GOLDTHWAIT, AND R.P. GOLDTHWAIT

1951 *The Geology of New Hampshire. Part I — Surficial Geology*. N.H. State Planning and Development Commission (reprinted 1963).

HAMMOND, A.L.

1971 "Mercury in the Environment: Natural and Human Values," *Science*, vol. 171, p. 788.

HUME, I.N.

1970 *A Guide to Artifacts of Colonial America*. Alfred A. Knopf, New York.

KINSEY, W.F. III

    1971   "The Middle Atlantic Culture Province: A Point of View," *Pennsylvania Archaeologist*, vol. 41, pp. 1-8.

    1972   *Archaeology in the Upper Delaware Valley: A Study of the Cultural Chronology of the Tocks Island Reservoir.* Pennsylvania Historical and Museum Commission, Anthropological Series no. 2.

KRAFT, H.C.

    1973   "The Plenge Site: A Paleo-Indian Occupation Site in New Jersey," *Archaeology of Eastern North America*, vol. 1, no. 1, pp. 56-117. Eastern States Archaeological Federation.

LENIG, D.

    1965   "The Oak Hill Horizon and its Relation to the Development of the Five Nations Iroquois Culture," *Researches and Transactions of the New York States Archaeological Association*, vol. 15, no. 1.

LEWIS, T.M.N., AND M. KNEBERG

    1959   "The Archaic Culture in the Middle South," *American Antiquity*, vol. 25, pp. 161-183.

MACDONALD, G.F.

    1968   *Debert: A Paleo-Indian Site in Central Nova Scotia.* Anthropological Papers, National Museum of Canada, no. 16.

MARSHALL, H.A.

    1942   "Some Ancient Indian Village Sites adjacent to Manchester, New Hampshire," *American Antiquity*, vol. 7, pp. 359-363.

MOOREHEAD, W.K.

    1931   *The Merrimack Archaeological Survey, a Preliminary Paper*, with supplementary notes on the Concord Valley by B.L. Smith. Peabody Museum, Salem.

MORSE, D.F.

    1973   "Dalton Culture in Northeast Arkansas," *Florida Anthropologist*, vol. 26, pp. 23-38.

POTTER, C.E.

    1856   *History of Manchester.* Manchester, N.H.

RITCHIE, W.A.

    1955   *Recent Discoveries Suggesting an Early Woodland Burial Cult in the Northeast.* New York State Museum and Science Service Circular, no. 40.

    1959   *The Stony Brook Site and its Relation to Archaic and Transitional Cultures on Long Island.* New York State Museum and Science Service Bulletin, 372.

1961   *A Typology and Nomenclature for New York Projectile Points.* New York State Museum and Science Service Bulletin, 384.

1969a   *The Archaeology of New York State.* (revised edition) Natural History Press.

1969b   *The Archaeology of Martha's Vineyard.* Natural History Press.

1971   *A Typology and Nomenclature for New York Projectile Points.* (revised edition) New York State Museum and Science Service Bulletin, 384.

1971a   "The Archaic in New York," *The Bulletin of the New York State Archaeological Association*, no. 52, pp. 2-12.

RITCHIE, W.A., AND R.E. FUNK

1971   "Evidence for Early Archaic Occupations on Staten Island," *Pennsylvania Archaeologist*, vol. 41, pp. 45-59.

RITCHIE, W.A., AND R.S. MACNEISH

1949   "The Pre-Iroquoian Pottery of New York State," *American Antiquity*, vol. 15, pp. 97-124.

SANGER, D., AND R.G. MACKAY

1973   "The Hirundo Archaeological Project — Preliminary Report," *Man in the Northeast*, no. 6, pp. 21-30.

SEMENOV, S.A.

1964   *Prehistoric Technology.* M.W. Thompson, translator. Barnes and Noble, Inc.

SIMMONS, C.S., W.H. LYFORD, JR., AND R. FEUER

1953   *Soil Survey of Hillsborough County, New Hampshire.* U.S. Department of Agriculture Soil Conservation Service, Series 1940, no. 13.

STAPLES, A.C., AND R.C. ATHEARN

1969   "The Bear Swamp Site: A Preliminary Report," *Bulletin of the Massachusetts Archaeological Society*, vol. 30, pp. 1-8.

VOSSBERG, W.A.

1959   "Comments on a Shawsheen River Site," *Bulletin of the Massachusetts Archaeological Society*, vol. 20, pp. 37-39.

WILLOUGHBY, C.C.

1935   *Antiquities of the New England Indians.* Peabody Museum of American Archaeology and Ethnology, Harvard University.

WILMSEN, E.N.

1968   "Functional Analysis of Flaked Stone Artifacts," *American Antiquity*, vol. 33, pp. 156-161.

WITTHOFT, J.

1955   "Early Archaic Complexes of Southeastern Pennsylvania," *Eastern States Archaeological Federation Bulletin*, no. 14, p. 13.

WOLLIN, G., D.B. ERICSON, AND M. EWING

1971   "Late Pleistocene Climates Recorded in Atlantic and Pacific Deep-Sea Sediments," in *The Late Cenozoic Glacial Ages*, K. Turekian, editor, pp. 199-214, Yale University Press.